10/04

MONOLOGUES IN DIALECT
FOR YOUNG ACTORS

A Smith and Kraus Book
Published by Smith and Kraus, Inc.
177 Lyme Road, Hanover, NH 03755

Cover and Text Design by Julia Gignoux, Freedom Hill Design

First Edition: April 2002
10 9 8 7 6 5 4 3 2 1

The Library of Congress Cataloging-In-Publication Data
Monologues in dialect for young actors / edited by Kimberly Mohne Hill.
p. cm. — (Young actors series)
Includes bibliographical references.
ISBN 1-57525-250-3
1. Monologues. 2. Acting. 3. English language—Dialects. 4. English language—Pronunciation by foreign speakers. I. Hill, Kimberly Mohne. II.Series.
PN2080 .M5473 2001
822.04508—dc21
    2001055038

MONOLOGUES IN DIALECT FOR YOUNG ACTORS

Edited by Kimberly Mohne Hill

YOUNG ACTORS SERIES

A SMITH AND KRAUS BOOK

FOR MY STUDENTS,
PAST, PRESENT, AND FUTURE,
AND MY MOM

CONTENTS

Note: The numbers in parentheses after titles show the number of selections from that title.

Section Four: American (New York)

Section Five: American (Southern)

DEEPENING CHARACTER THROUGH DIALECT

As an instructor of dialects at the American Conservatory Theater (A.C.T.), I have found that young actors are especially adept at the creation and application of dialects with their characters. There seems to be a sense of abandon in young actors where their voice and speech is concerned, and they seem to enjoy the instant gratification they feel when they observe such a strong difference in their own vocal patterns. Dialects can instantly transform you into another person by affecting the very essence of who you are to the world — your speech. Dialects, for many actors, are enjoyable, useful tools.

The students at A.C.T. are taught that dialects are not to be taken lightly, as some silly voices they put on to "be different." Just as the essence of who you are is revealed in your personal speech pattern, so are your characters' souls revealed in *their* speech patterns. Dialects are to be respected. We study the region of the dialect to understand its place and its context. This deeper understanding makes us take responsibility for creating as true and realistic and deep a dialect as we possibly can. We strive to move beyond stereotype and generality.

After the students have researched the dialect and the region in which it occurs, they listen to tapes and study the actual sound changes that occur in the dialect. Through practice sentences and improvisations, they begin to feel the difference of the sounds in their bodies, and they work to feel free in the dialect, attempting to develop a personal attachment to the sounds they are making so that the dialect becomes a necessity for their characters rather than an option. Then they work with scenes and monologues.

The monologues represented in this collection are not necessarily written *in* a particular dialect; but rather, serve to give the actor a feel for the rhythm, emotion, society, or history of the *people* or *place* of the dialect being studied. These monologues will work when you speak them in dialect, but they may not necessarily have been written specifically for performance in dialect.

The introductions to the scenes have been written to help the readers learn and apply the dialect of the section. The dialect of a character is directly related to who they are in the world and what their world has been all their lives. In this regard, approach each dialect as a character study. Find out where your character lives — not just a town on a map, but the buildings in the town, the weather of the town, the people of the town, etc. Find out what country the character lives in and what cultural, social, historical, geographical, and religious influences the country has experienced. Find out about the education level and social circle of your character. Find out about your character's dreams and fears, challenges, and triumphs. All these "character" questions are actually the way to develop a strong, nonstereotypical dialect. You become invested in the way you speak because you know your character has no other choice but to speak in the way he or she always has. You are not simply putting on a funny accent and trying to make it seem real, it *is* real, because it is who you are in this monologue/world/play.

As you begin to speak the dialects aloud, it is important to remember that you are a human being, and that your speech is as malleable as your mind. Most likely, you have found yourself in the position of talking with someone who has a real dialect, and by accident, you find yourself slipping into it. That is normal! If it happens to you, speaking the native dialect *you* speak, of course it can happen to your characters when they speak their native dialects. I am giving you permission to be not perfect at these dialects. Speech is not a perfect science. Speech (and dialect) is ever changing, depending on the speaker and the person speaking to the speaker. So approach this work with a lightness of heart and tongue, and you will be fine!

Of course, there are some basic precepts that need to be maintained when speaking a dialect. Just as you have permission to be not perfect at the dialect at hand, you must always remain consistent. Consistency in dialect means that when you pronounce a word a certain way, take a proper name for example, you *always* pronounce it that way. Sometimes your stage directions will tell you to pronounce something in a certain way, just so that another character can later correct you. Consistency also means maintaining the flavor and rhythm of your dialect even when the others onstage are speaking in different dialects. This is probably one of the hardest things to do as an actor, but the stronger your character research is, the stronger your connection to your dialect will be; and even if you slip into someone else's dialect onstage, your character can justify it!

I have included in each section a reference source to help actors find the actual sounds of the dialect being studied. It is important to listen to as many primary sources of the dialects as possible to get an idea of how it sounds aloud. Seeing the sound changes on a page can only do so much, you must hear and see real people speaking the sounds.

For those students who know the International Phonetic Alphabet (IPA), I have left a space beside each of the phonetically spelled sound changes for you to mark the IPA equivalent.

In the Appendix are improvisations and exercises I have found effective in getting students to free themselves of the head work that comes from drilling sounds off a page — the improvisations allow them to play with the sounds and characters in their bodies, under the safe umbrella of acting and play. Everything they do is right and accepted; every sound they make is correct. With this freedom comes confidence in their ability to speak the dialect and create real, truthful "regionally enhanced" characters. Some of the improvs can be used with any of the dialects, and some work best only with the dialects described. Some of the improvisations work best with groups, and some are private, personal exercises. All are fun!

SECTION ONE
BRITISH
(STANDARD AND COCKNEY)

STANDARD BRITISH INTRODUCTION

American actors are fortunate that the study of the British dialect is made easier because so many British films are shown in American movie theaters and are available in video stores. We need only rent a Merchant-Ivory film to hear and see the British world right in our living rooms. We can practice imitating a British actor by rewinding the videotape and repeating the actor's lines over and over until our mimicry has made it "just right" in our mouths. However, this is only one beginning step in the quest for authentic British characters — we have much deeper work to do in order to do our characters justice.

Most American actors will have to do Standard British (also called Received Pronunciation, London, or BBC) at some point in their careers. An incredible amount of amazing British theatrical literature and wonderful classic British characters keep American audiences challenged and entertained, calling for American actors to take command of the British rhythm and sounds.

For our purposes, we will be focusing on the sound changes and elements of Standard British spoken by the relatively educated, neutral London population. I use the term *neutral* not in the political sense, but in the sense that there are no regional enhancements to the general speech pattern we will study. The education system in Great Britain is such that, even with a bare minimum of education, elocution will have been taught at some point. Also, the BBC national news and other forms of visual and audio media will use a general, nonregional accent, and this carries over to the listeners. As with all forms of language, this is evolving, and more and more Britons are laying claim to their original regional dialects.

It is important to know that there exists in Britain (and indeed in each area of dialect we will study) a wide variety of dialects that are based on the region's economic, social, and geographic conditions. For example, the Northumberland region of England, the farm country remoteness, coupled with the presence of the nearby Scottish border creates a speech pattern that can sound completely different than the one heard in London. As an actor, it is up to you to find out where your character is from and research the dialect needs of that particular region.

Standard British dialect is called English for a reason: They invented the language! Of course, it takes its roots from a variety of sources, but the finished product is a form of speech that we tend to consider a heightened form of American English. The sounds tend to be more precisely made, but with an ease and sense of confidence that comes from having spoken the language since its creation.

The people of England are class-conscious and focus intently on their speech as a symbol of their status in the community at large. Even in Standard British, there are some people who are higher status and some who are less so, both qualities being exhibited in their speech.

What follows are some key points about Standard British and the important sound changes/elements.

- As an American (Californian) actor doing a British accent, I have noticed that I must make my mouth rounder than it normally is — indeed, when I look at British people speaking, the corners of their mouths seem to come close together in an almost frowning way. That is not to say that British people do not smile — they do — but the placement of their sound has an element of roundness to it quite consistently.
- A precision about the British sounds requires some conscious effort, but must appear to be completely easy and relaxed when we speak.
- If a word is unimportant in a sentence (usually articles, conjunctions, pronouns, linking verbs), the British barely give it any notice at all. They go for the image words and the operative (important) words of the sentence, which helps with the British rhythm.
- The British dialect stresses only one syllable per word, even if the word has more than one syllable. For example, we (in California) say "SEK ra tair ree" (secretary), and they would say "SEK reh trih." We tend to pay attention to every syllable of a word, and they focus on the stressed syllable only.
- The tone/sound of the British dialect uses the forward muscles of the face (rounded lips), but there is great openness and roundness at the base of the tongue near the throat — imagine the sounds coming out already formed perfectly way down in the center of your body.
- Even though the British dialect has a different inflection rhythm when they ask a question (they tend to raise the pitch and inflection on the second to last word in the sentence, i.e., "Do you WANT some?"), it's important to keep the inflection under check so as not to become too sing-song. Just remind yourself to *mean* what you say.
- Try not to smile, and practice over-rounding your lips when you first begin playing with the sound changes.

- We *like* hearing them talk. There is a reason for that. They know how to make speech sound good, eloquent, and flawless. There is power to that awareness — you can *know* people will listen to you!
- Please do not use your new British dialect on Shakespeare (unless directed to). It is a "bad acting" cliché.

STANDARD BRITISH FILM, TELEVISION, AND AUDIO REFERENCES

FILM

Mansfield Park	Cast
Four Weddings and a Funeral, Notting Hill	Hugh Grant
The Sound of Music, Victor/Victoria, Mary Poppins, Thoroughly Modern Millie	Julie Andrews
Sense and Sensibility	Cast
Hamlet (Film and CD)	Kenneth Branagh's version
Shakespeare in Love	Dame Judi Dench, Joseph Fiennes, Gwyneth Paltrow
A Room with a View, Howard's End, Remains of the Day (Merchant-Ivory films)	Cast
Mrs. Dalloway	Cast
Truly, Madly, Deeply	Juliet Stevenson, Alan Rickman
The Princess Bride	Cary Elwes, Robin Wright
Sliding Doors, Emma	Gwyneth Paltrow
Dirty Rotten Scoundrels	Michael Caine
Arthur (I and II)	Dudley Moore, John Gielgud
Milo and Otis	Dudley Moore
Bedknobs and Broomsticks	Angela Lansbury, Roddy McDowell
The Parent Trap, Pollyanna	Hayley Mills

DIALECT TAPES AND BOOKS

(These tapes and books are available through Drama Books or Samuel French or in the libraries of any university with a theater department)

Standard British	Gilian Lane-Plescia
Stage Dialects	Jerry Blunt
English Accents and Dialects	Hughes and Trudgill
Dialects for the Stage	Evangeline Machlin
Acting with an Accent, Standard British	David Alan Stern
IDEA website	www.ukans.edu/~idea/index.html

For a more complete and detailed list of films/resources, see Ginny Kopf's book The Dialect Handbook.

Standard British
Elements and Sounds

- The dropped *r:* The British dialect drops the *r* sound at the ends of words and when the *r* precedes a consonant. The *uh* you see in the substitutions below is actually really subtle. It's a little off-glide of sound. Pay attention to the first part of the change (the pure vowel) and the rest should take care of itself. If you overdo the *uh* sound, you will go to a Brooklyn dialect, so be careful! Keep the essence of *r* in there and pretend you are still saying it.

ear → ih uh	here, we're, dear → hih uh, wih uh, dih uh
air → eh uh	where, their, fare → weh uh, theh uh, feh uh
oor → oo uh	sure, boor, moor → shoo uh, boo uh, moo uh
ore → oh uh	you're, more, door → yoh uh, moh uh, doh uh
are → ah	far, car, yard → fah, kah, yahd
er → eh	girl, word, heard → gehl, wehd, hehd

- The round sounds: These will take some effort and an ear for you to hear the difference. Most Americans do not make these sounds naturally (except Brooklyn New Yorkers) and so you will have to retrain your mouth and your mind to get them to be natural. You must really round your lips and drop your jaw open (two fingers wide) to shape these sounds, but remember to imagine the sound coming from the center of your body already perfectly formed.

  ah → aw (rounded almost to an *oh* sound)
  > law, all, fall hall → law, awl, fawl, hawl

  ah → o (rounded and "popped" like the sound in the word "pop")
  > hot, top, stop → hot, top, stop

  ow → ah oh   how, now, brown → hahoh, nahoh, brahohn
  oh → uh oh   go, slow, road, show → guhoh, sluhoh,
  > ruhohd, shuhoh

- The liquid *u:* Much the way the word "music" has a *y* sound after the consonant "m," the British dialect inserts a *y* sound before the long *u* sound after the letters *t, d,* and *n.* Note: if the word has an *o* in the spelling, do not use the liquid *u.*
  Duke, duty, dubious → Dyuke, dyuty, dyubious

new, nude, newer → nyew, nyude, nyewer

tune, Tuesday, tutor → tyune, Tyuesday, tyutor

- The pure Anne sound: The short *a* in the word *Anne* (and others) can tend to be flattened and blended into the consonant that changes the *a* into an *ay* sometimes. In the British dialect, you must pay attention to the vowel (all vowels) before you move on to the consonant. The *a* sound is made with a wide open, smiling mouth (like you are biting into an apple). Make the vowel sound purely, and *then* say the consonant that follows it.

Anne, can, and → A nne, ka n, a nd

- Prefixes: Keeping with the tradition of stressing only one syllable in a word, the British dialect uses the pure, short sound *ih* on prefixes/suffixes (where we, especially in California, would say *ee*).

believe, prepare, rehearse → bih lieve, prih pare, rih hearse

- Suffixes: When words end with *ed, y,* or *ly,* the British dialect will not stress it or make it a full *ee* or *ed* sound, but will rather substitute the precise *ih* sound instead.

wanted, lovely, wordy → wan tihd, love lih, wuh dih

- The voiced *th*: In the word *with*, the British dialect voices the *th* sound (like in the word *this*).

- The ask list: One of the main errors made by American actors learning the British dialect is the overuse of the *ah* sound whenever a word is spelled with an *a*. The "ahsk list" seeks to eliminate that tendency by listing all the words that substitute the *ah* sound instead of the *a* sound. If it is not on the list, use the pure Anne sound. For the complete ask list, see pages 81 to 83 of *Speak with Distinction.* by Skinner, Mansell, and Monich.

STANDARD BRITISH
PRACTICE SENTENCES

ear → ih uh:

Here dear, the cheer is near to tears. We're fearful of deers.

air → eh uh:

Where there is care, share the fare. The lair of the bear is fairly scary.

oor → oh uh:

The poor do-er of newer sewers was sure pure. Fewer pure boors swim moors.

ore → oh uh (very rounded):

The door was shorter than before the war. More than the four lowered the floor.

are → ah:

Park your car and start your heart. The part of the art was hard to cart.

er → eh:

The girl's birth was the first in the world. Hurl the churl to the earth.

ah → aw (very rounded):

All the tall law books fall in the hall. Always call after the Ball.

ah → o (rounded and popped):

The hot copper coffee pots popped their tops. Not in the pot, Colin!

ow → ah oh:

How now brown cow? Round and round without a sound, they found the ground.

uh → uh oh:

Don't go to the road show, it's slow. Joe and Rose know the flow of the crow.

Pure Anne:

Anne can stand to fan with her hand the man's back. Plan to scram.

Liquid *u:*

Tuesday, the Duke and the Tutor played new tunes on the Tuba.

Prefixes:

The rehearsal was believed to be preparing the delivery of delight.

Suffixes:

It's lovely and sunny in the newly renovated terrace. Calmly study the Wanted List.

COCKNEY BRITISH

Most students of dialect have a good deal of fun with the Cockney British dialect. Just as American actors can relax their speech a little to create the essence of a Southern dialect, so too can we relax our British dialect a bit to create the Cockney sounds.

The Cockney dialect is an evolving dialect. Historically attributed to undereducated, working-class people from the crowded lower suburbs of London, the Cockney sounds have been making an appearance in the speech patterns of some prominent and highly educated British citizens (namely, the current Prime Minister, Tony Blair). Much as street slang in America finds its way into the general speech patterns of *all* races and classes, the Cockney sounds contain the same allure and hip qualities people like to sprinkle throughout their speech. It's fun. It's accessible. It makes one seem more as if one belongs to the group.

The Cockney dialect was originally so deeply ingrained in the Cockney people, that it made them completely unintelligible to the upper-class citizens of nearby London proper — and that is the way the Cockneys wanted it. Almost in direct rebellion against their more privileged neighbors, the Cockneys would maintain their distinctive dialect to create a sense of separate identity and status over the stuffy, aristocratic Londoners who looked down on them. They went so far in their plan to distance themselves from the Standard British speakers that they created what is still called "rhyming slang" — a secret code language that only they know.

Using words and phrases that rhymed with what they meant to say (i.e., "apples and pears" for "stairs," sometimes shortened to "apple"), the Cockneys could communicate in a mystifying language. While not as prevalent among the greater speakers of Cockney nowadays, the rhyming slang can still be observed among the wholesale grocers, traders, and workers is specialized areas of industrial London. (The PBS documentary *The History of English* contains great samples of this particular speech pattern.)

When an upper-class or middle-class Briton speaks with the elements of the Cockney dialect, the dialect they speak moves toward what is now being called Estuary English. If your character needs a British dialect with a hint of working-class, Cockney elements, chances are you will be speaking Estuary English. To do a true Cockney dialect on stage would make you almost entirely unintelligible, and that is not what you want to do!

If you do all the sound changes and elements that follow at the same time, you will have a strong Cockney dialect. Use just a few key sounds and you will have a slightly working-class version of the General British accent — Estuary English. Have fun!

- Like New Yorkers, you will find in a later section, the Cockney people have a certain energy of attack on words and phrases — the energy of living in a crowded, bustling metropolitan area.
- The Cockneys are a proud group of people who are devoted to maintaining a sense of themselves and their traditions. To give over to the standardized British pronunciation of words would seem to the proud Cockneys something of a sellout.
- Whereas the Standard British sounds are produced by a rounding of the mouth and a dropping of the resonance into the chest and throat, the Cockney sounds are much flatter in the back of the mouth and resonate in the nose.
- As mentioned before, true Cockney can be fast, mumbled, and almost totally unintelligible — be careful.
- There are more sound changes and substitutions in this dialect than in the Standard British, so you must concentrate on maintaining a sense of what the original word is. For example, when you say "wiv" instead of the word "with," we must still know what you meant to say. Keep thinking of the original word and its correct spelling, that way you still keep an essence of the correct pronunciation, and we can then understand you.
- There is a sense of mischief in the Cockney dialect that comes through in the way you carry yourself. It is much more relaxed than the Standard British. It can be cool and hip.
- Cockneys have little lip movement, but the vowels stay rounded and the sounds come out of a more open mouth.
- Like Eliza Doolittle in the film *My Fair Lady,* there can be a tendency to drag out operative syllables of words: "gaaaooohhh ooonnn" ("go on"). Again, it's very nasalized and whiny sounding.
- Cockneys are not quiet.

COCKNEY BRITISH FILM, TELEVISION, AND AUDIO REFERENCES

FILMS

The Very Thought of You	All levels of British
Beautiful People	Multiple levels throughout cast
The Limey	Terence Stamp
Monty Python and the Holy Grail,	
Monty Python and the Meaning of Life	Cast
My Fair Lady	Eliza and her father
Oliver	Cast
Chitty Chitty Bang Bang	Most of the cast
Remains of the Day	Anthony Hopkins's father
Willy Wonka and the Chocolate Factory	Cast
A Fish Called Wanda	Michael Palin

TELEVSION
"East Enders"

DIALECT TAPES AND BOOKS
(Available through Drama Books, Samuel French, or any library of a university with a theater department.)

Cockney for Actors	Gillian Lane-Plescia
Stage Dialects	Jerry Blunt
English with an Accent	BBC Record
Dialects for the Stage	Evangeline Machlin
Acting with an Accent (Cockney)	David Alan Stern

COCKNEY BRITISH
ELEMENTS AND SOUNDS

- The dropped *r* and the intrusive *r*: As with the British dialect, the Cockneys drop the *r* at the ends of words and before consonants. When a word ends with an *r* and the next word starts with a vowel ("car and driver"), they will pronounce that final *r*. Sometimes, this rule makes them overcompensate on words that do not have an *r* in the spelling, and they will accidentally put one in there ("law and order" would become "lawr and ohduh"). This is called an intrusive *r*.
- They always use the liquid *u:*
  Duke, new, tune → dyuke, nyu, tyun
- They drop the *h* at the beginnings of words. Be careful not to make a "glottal attack" (slamming your vocal chords together on the initial vowel of the word), and say the word as if you are silently producing the *h*.
  Harry, he, hit → 'arry, 'ee, 'it
- They drop the *g* on *-ing* endings.
  running, flying, walking → runnin', floyin', walkin'
- The consonant combination *th* changes to either *v* or *f* depending on whether it is voiced or unvoiced.
  mother, father these → muvvuh, fahvuh, veez
  thanks, both, Goth → fanks, buhohf, Gof
- The final *l* in words is not done with the tongue against the roof of the mouth, but rather with a shaping of the lips into almost an *oo* sound (think Elmer Fudd).
  well, bill, careful → weh oo, bi oo, keh foo
- Unique and important to the Cockney dialect is the glottal stop (symbol is ʔ): Instead of your articulators (tongue, teeth, lips) coming together to make a sound (the consonant *t* or *k*), your throat does a little catch and you pretend to have made the sound. In simple terms, you are dropping the *t* and *k* sound in certain instances. The glottal stop only happens when the *t* is in the middle of two vowel sounds, or at the end of a word, and when the *k* sound is at the end of a word.
  little, late, bit, glottal → liʔoo, lyʔ, biʔ, gloʔoo
  like, lake, make → loyʔ, lyʔ, myʔ

- The [ay] (long a) sound becomes [eye] and will be represented with a [y] like in the word [my].

  take, may, gray, paper → ty?, my, gry, pypuh
- The [y/eye] sound becomes [oy].

  while, kite, fly, my → woyl, koy?, floy, moy
- The pure Anne sound (a) becomes very nasalized and can almost become an [eh] sound.

  man, stand, ran → man/mehn, stand/stend, ran/ren
- The [oh] sound gets an open glide into it so it becomes almost like [a-oh].

  go, show, no → ga-oh, sha-oh, na-oh
- The [ow] sound becomes more nasalized and sounds like [ah-ow].

  how, now, brown → hah-ow, nah-ow, brah-own
- The [ee] (long e) sound becomes [ay]. Remember to keep the essence of the real word you are saying in there.

  he, me, free → 'ay, may, fray
- The [eh] sound becomes a lazier [ih] sound.

  get, them, dens → gi?, vim, dinz
- The [aw] sound becomes *very* rounded and sounds almost like [ooaw].

  all, law, fall, call → ooawl, looaw, fooawl, cooawl
- The pure [oo] sounds get a lazy schwa glide into it so it becomes [uh-oo].

  blue, grew, food → bluhoo, gruhoo, fuhood

COCKNEY BRITISH
PRACTICE SENTENCES

[ay] → [y]:

The rain in Spain stays mainly in the plain. They came from the same place.

[y/eye] → [oy]:

While I was flying, my wife left in the night. Liza likes to fight the right battle.

[oh] → [a-oh]:

I told the old goat to grow the gold coat. The boat is slow for the rowers and Joe.

[ow] → nasalized [ah-ow]:

The cow of the town was brown around the crown. They found them downtown.

[ee] → [ay]:

We three better see if the meat is free. The tree pleases me.

[eh] → [ih]:

Get them in the den with the men of Trent. The kennel of leopards is second to none.

[aw] → very rounded [ooaw]:

They fall all over Paul when he calls. I thought the law was fraught with awful rules.

[oo] → [uh-oo]:

The blue shoe is for the youth movement. They threw the computer off the roof.

[h] dropped:

Harry was his biggest hero. The heckler got his hand chopped off by Horace.

[g] dropped on [-ing] endings:

Getting off the rolling bus was scaring me. The laughing hyenas were boring.

[th] → [f/v]:

Me mother was thinking of thanking me father. This is something.

[l] in final position:

Well, Bill, the little call to the hall will tell you. They can tell if the spell is well.

[ʔ] the glottal stop:

With a little bit of kittle, the cake will be better. The glottal stop is a little bit of fun.

ALMOST GROWN
by Richard Cameron

Cockney British: Female

THE PLAY: The events of childhood are revealed to have lasting impacts on three young men. We see their lives play out in their late teens as they take their separate paths, but we are also swept back to the days when they were careless schoolboys playing practical jokes on classmates. A tragic twist of fate brings the former friends face-to-face once more.

THE MONOLOGUE: Elaine (12) is speaking from her coma. She was hit by a car driven by the object of her crush, Scott. Her accident has altered or destroyed the lives around her while she has remained oblivious in a coma. This monologue will be played as if the actress were just as awake and alive as all of the other characters around her. There is no need for a dreamlike presentation.

TIME AND PLACE: Present. Darkness. England.

Fade out. In the dark.

ELAINE: Was I little then? Was it yesterday? Or years ago? Not little, no. Never had Sorrow then. He came when I was twelve. Yes. How old am I now? Still twelve? Is this a dream I'm dreaming that same day night, that Saturday, or is this a memory of me then? Me. Elaine. Am I grown old? Who am I now?
(Lights up on Elaine. She continues.)
Saturday. Sunday. The grass is high and buzzing. Sorrow hears me call his name. His ears come up and then his head. I call again and he sees me. Comes across the field corner to corner, waits for me to walk the track. Shudders in the sunlight. Nuzzles in my neck. I love you, Sorrow. His eyes love me back. Black eyes. All day. All the long day down, across the fields and lanes, he takes me down the long lanes. Strong, shuddering, safe. Together in the world, ours, and precious, and now.

And then that noise, that sudden sound that sends you up and scared and skidding across the track. A car. Only a little car. Can't see it over the hedge yet, beyond the bend, but there, coming. Roaring. I can't hold you now. You're out of me now it's here. The wheels, the windscreen, those two faces. His face. Her face. His face behind the wheel. A face seeing my face, seeing each other's fear, and Sorrow knows my fear and his own, goes up and back, and I go.

(The lights begin to fade.)

I'm falling. Falling into the front of the car and far away I hear the sounds . . . voices . . . doors banging . . .a soothing voice . . . a frightened voice . . . inside . . . inside a . . . moving . . . lights passing . . . corridors . . . crying . . . somebody crying.

This is a dream I don't want. Wake me up. Wake me up from this. Take me back to Saturdays and Sorrow. Please. Please God.

(Lights out.)
(In the dark.)

GOODNIGHT CHILDREN, EVERYWHERE
by Richard Nelson

Standard British: Female

THE PLAY: During World War II, some families in England sent their children to the United States or Canada to protect them from the bombing of English cities. The title of the play is taken from the words of a popular song of the time that was used to close each of the evening radio shows as a prayer of sorts for the displaced children. Now, after the war, a family welcomes home the last child to return, a now 17-year-old only brother in a family of all girls. The changes in the women and the startling growth in their brother only serve to exacerbate the unresolved emotions surrounding their experiences in the war and the effect it had on their family.

THE MONOLOGUE: Ann (20) is the oldest and most settled of the family. She has married a successful doctor and is pregnant with her first child. The return of her brother stirs up her feelings of discontent and confusion as she faces the facts of her well-planned life.

TIME AND PLACE: Late Spring, 1945. A large flat in Clapham, South London.

ANN: *(Quietly.)* *(She turns to Peter, then turns away and stands.)* So . . . I hate Mike.
  (Peter looks at her.)
  You heard him. Sometimes I hate him. And sometimes I say to myself, you shouldn't stay with someone you hate. And I believe that. *(Shrugs. She picks up Mike's teacup.)* Tea?
  (Peter shakes his head. Ann starts to head off for the kitchen, then returns right away.)
  Father used to do that to me. *(Beat.)* I remember once, he had a taxi waiting. I helped him down with his bag. He let me. He helped me help him. And as he was getting in — after a glance at the ticking meter? He said, "Ann, I've decided which school you're going to." Then taxi door slam and he was gone. No discussion. Nothing. *(Beat.)* Like you're a — thing to be told. Like you are nothing. *(Beat.)* I'm going to clean today. You can help me. Move the chairs around, that sort of thing. *(Short*

pause.) It's because of you that Mike's looking for another flat. Suddenly we're — "crowded." *(Beat.)* All I ask is for the opportunity to talk about things. Before decisions are made. Before things are done and can't be — reversed. *(She looks at Peter.)* You are so young. I can't believe how young you are. *(Beat.)* So what are we going to do today? Should we talk about it? *(Short pause.)* I love this flat. I must know every inch. *(Pointing to the sofa.)* I remember — God knows how old I was — certainly not old enough to "get it" — but I came around that corner. And there was Mother and Father on that sofa. Right there, Peter. Her blouse was — it was hanging off her shoulder. She was sitting on Dad. *(Beat.)* The upholstery is the same as it was then. We haven't changed it. *(Beat.)* I'm not going to the pictures with you. I've stopped all that. You can go yourself if you want. *(Short pause. She thinks, then:)* You step outside today — just one foot out of your home — and it all makes no sense anymore. And it's been building up to this for a while. *(Suddenly remembers.)* About a month ago, I was out — you know the shop — it used to be a greengrocer's near the surgery on the High Street? Of course you don't know it. Well, it's reopened. And do you know what they're selling — the only thing they are selling as far as I could tell? Crows. Dead crows. Rows and rows and rows of hanging black crows. They're selling them — to eat, I think. *(Beat.)* Go and have a look if you like. Quite a sight. *(Short pause. She comes and sits next to him, takes his hand, puts it on her stomach.)* It's kicking. *(Her mind drifts away, to:)* You try and make sense —. You start to ask yourself — should I do this? Should I do that? *(Beat.)* You have such a wonderful smell about you. *(She takes his hand and holds it.)* We're all alone. *(Pause. She suddenly stands.)* I need to go for a pee. Excuse me.

GOODNIGHT CHILDREN, EVERYWHERE
by Richard Nelson

Standard British: Female

THE PLAY: During World War II, some families in England sent their children to the United States or Canada to protect them from the bombing of English cities. The title of the play is taken from the words of a popular song of the time that was used to close each of the evening radio shows as a prayer of sorts for the displaced children. Now, after the war, a family welcomes home the last child to return, a now 17-year-old only brother in a family of all girls. The changes in the women and the startling growth in their brother only serve to exacerbate the unresolved emotions surrounding their experiences in the war and the effect it had on their family.

THE MONOLOGUE: Vi (19) is the actress of the family. She is the carrier of the stories, the family's history. As she observes the far-too intimate relationship developing between her sister and brother, she recounts the horrors she observed during the war, as if by telling it, she could somehow make her brother feel the way she felt.

TIME AND PLACE: Late Spring, 1945. A large flat in Clapham, South London.

VI: Leave our brother alone. He's not a child. We don't have to keep fawning over him.
(They look at each other. Then Vi turns away.)
(Turning away.) Leave him alone. What were we talking about? The day Mother died. I was just talking about the day Mother died. I walked out of the woods, a little bloody, and Mum's dead. We're not the sisters you left. Are we, Ann? So much happened. There's so much Peter doesn't know about. So much he's missed. *(Beat.)* There was that woman. Weeks? Months later? After Mother's death, Father comes to visit us — with a woman. What was her name?
(No response from Ann.)

We never wrote to you about any of this. And the most remarkable thing was that she looked like Mother. Like a rather blurry carbon copy of Mother. Wouldn't you agree?

(Peter looks at Ann.)

We look at her — we didn't know what to say. Father's got his arm around her. They hold hands. What am I to feel? Do I love her? Do I hate her? She tried — to be nice. At supper that night she was very nice. Then we went for a walk in the morning. Just "us girls." *(Beat.)* And we learned, didn't we, that she was obsessed with Mother. With things she'd heard — been told —.

Lies. How Mother had been so mean with some things —

And positively extravagant when it came to other things — for herself. Shoes. How many shoes? That was not true! He was lying to her about Mother! Mother bought maybe three pairs of shoes at one time only because she had such narrow feet that when she found shoes that fitted her, which was rare! — she bought a few pairs! That makes sense. Doesn't it make sense? That doesn't make her a spendthrift. That doesn't make her selfish for God's sake!! She kept every damn shoe she ever bought and dyed them over and over and over! This wasn't our mother, woman! I know it sounds petty, but I can still see that face, that almost-mother's face, how I wanted to slap that face as she said, I remember every word, as she took my hand on that walk and said: "It seems your mother wasn't a very kind woman. How hard that must have been for you. Still, I'm sure she tried to love you in her own way." *(Short pause.)* We're weak, Peter. We've become very weak. *(To Ann.)* Leave him alone.

(Ann looks to Peter.)

GOODNIGHT CHILDREN, EVERYWHERE
by Richard Nelson

Standard British: Female

THE PLAY: During World War II, some families in England sent their children to the United States or Canada to protect them from the bombing of English cities. The title of the play is taken from the words of a popular song of the time that was used to close each of the evening radio shows as a prayer of sorts for the displaced children. Now, after the war, a family welcomes home the last child to return, a now 17-year-old only brother in a family of all girls. The changes in the women and the startling growth in their brother only serve to exacerbate the unresolved emotions surrounding their experiences in the war and the effect it had on their family.

THE MONOLOGUE: Vi (19) is the actress of the family. She is the carrier of the stories, the family's history. Peter knows nothing of the lives his sisters led while he was tucked away safe in Canada. Vi shares the story of his journey away from them.

TIME AND PLACE: Late Spring, 1945. A large flat in Clapham, South London.

VI: Stay in here.
(Peter sits back down. Beat.)
(Ignoring him.) They wouldn't let anyone — go after that. You were the last. *(Beat.)* We waited a full week wondering what had happened. If it had been your ship. *(Beat.)* We thought then we might have lost you. I even imagined, sitting in the bath, what it would have been like, felt like — to drown. And to float to the bottom of the sea. Like a leaf, I thought, as it falls. We cried ourselves to sleep. *(Beat.)* The first newspaper accounts said that the little boys had stood in perfect lines, all straight, all calm. Betty said that surely meant you couldn't be on that ship, our little Peter couldn't ever stand still. *(She smiles at Peter, then:)* For a week we held our breath. And then we heard. You were in Canada. You were lucky. How we celebrated! Mum and Dad and Betty and Ann and me. How happy we were that our Peter was safe. I'd never known a

happier day. *(She picks up the photo again.)* I began to dream you were coming home. *(Beat.)* Then, finally, you really were coming home. *(She sets the photo back down.)* Now you're home. *(She stands. Calls.)* Betty, I'll help you with that dress!

(She heads down the hallway. Peter sits alone on the sofa.)

GREAT EXPECTATIONS
by Charles Dickens; adapted by John Clifford

Standard British: Female

THE PLAY: In a dramatization of Dickens' famous novel, colorful and dramatic characters weave in and out of Pip's life in a rapid pace. True to the novel, Pip goes from extreme poverty to extreme wealth and back again in his quest for the truth about his life and the life of his love, Estella.

THE MONOLOGUE: Estella (19 to 21) has grown up and is even more beautiful than Pip remembered. Seeing her again at a ball, he falls more in love with her. She tries to convince him that it will never work due to the person she was raised to be — a person with no love to give.

TIME AND PLACE: Victorian England. Evening. A ball in London.

ESTELLA: *(To Pip.)* Do you think it is a pleasure to be brought up to be admired?
Do you think that in itself is sufficient? Pip, you are so taken up with yourself. Have you noticed nothing?
Do you not know her story? Did you never take the trouble to enquire?
You think she's away, Pip, and safely locked up.
There in her dead dark room in the cobwebs and dust.
But I cannot leave her. Nor can she leave me.
She walks through the halls in her shroud like a ghost.
I have to write to her each night.
A long letter, Pip, telling her of my conquests.
And you don't know why. Pip, Pip. You are blind.

She had everything. Her father loved her.
But she was orphaned, Pip, while she was still young.
She was rich, Pip, and very lovely, and all alone.
Satis House was a grand place then, she told me.
Full of laughter and sunlight. At night,
The candles in the parties shone like stars.
As they do here, Pip.

One night she met a man at the Midsummer ball.
A tall man, he was, and handsome and dark.
They danced all night long as they do in the stories
And when dawn came, and it was over, and the candles were
Tired and pale,
She was still fresh and overflowing with laughter
And could have danced the whole night all over again.
The wedding was fixed. It was to be a grand affair.
The most beautiful wedding that was ever seen.
The dress was bought, the guests were invited
She was putting on the most beautiful silk gown.

[and then the letter came] It was brought by one of her servants.

It broke off the wedding. It told her she was worthless.
It told her she'd been useful for the money
But marriage was a joke.

She sat all day in her dress, holding the letter
And that night sent for Jaggers. She had read his name in the papers.

She laid the place to waste.
And then she found me.

You see, Pip, like you, I never knew who I was.
All I remember is a dark room in a dark house.
And a sad lady looking down on me.

I was brought up to be admired.
You have heard her,
Heard her say it. Brought up to be admired.
To be gawped at, Pip. To be smelt and pawed at.
And why do you think that was?

Fool. It was for her revenge!

THE GUT GIRLS
by Sarah Daniels

Cockney British: Female

THE PLAY: Set in Deptford in the turn of the century (1899–1900), *The Gut Girls* is a play about the lives of young women who worked in the meat processing plants. Contrasting the Victorian ideals of manners and gentility, the lives of the gut girls were bawdy and difficult. When a local Duchess undertakes to reform and refine the girls by training them at a club she sets up for them, their lives change immeasurably.

THE MONOLOGUE: Annie (16) is the newest member of the "gut girls" (women who disemboweled the butchered animals at the local processing plant) and has a secret that has weighed heavily on her. Ellen takes it upon herself to befriend the new girl and get her a better life.

TIME AND PLACE: Turn-of-the-century (1899–1900) England. Deptford. Ellen's room. After work.

ANNIE: I was in service, oh, not round here, no, in a beautiful house in Blackheath, and I was real proud of meself, oh, I was. The master and mistress was all right, never thrashed you or anything, they was above that. Had a son at Oxford University, really nice spoken, educated gentleman. When he came home in the holiday, he wouldn't let me be. In front of anybody, I mean, he treated me like dirt, but would creep up on me when no one was about. I fought him. I pleaded with him, I threatened him, but he'd laugh. His mama would never believe it of her darling son. Oh, and I wasn't the only one, and it didn't only happen once and when I fell, that was it — got shot of me. I 'ad nowhere ter go, nowhere. I walked the streets and I was was picked up and taken to be examined — six months gone I was — for diseases; to them I was a prostitute and the way they treat you and the way they look at you, and the way they hate you, and the way they blame you and everyone blames me. But I never cried, not one of them saw me cry and when I got to that home, it was awful but it was heaven. And even when I was told it was dead I never cried. Why don't they tell you birth is such an awful, bloody, terrible, painful thing. It was born with the cord round its neck. It had strangled itself the poor, poor, little tiny thing and I looked at it before they took it away and I thought, you lucky, lucky bastard, how much better if I'd have been born like that.

(She starts to sob for the first time since the baby was born. Ellen looks at her and puts her arms round her and lets her cry.)

THE GUT GIRLS
by Sarah Daniels

Cockney British: Female

THE PLAY: Set in Deptford in the turn of the century (1899–1900), *The Gut Girls* is a play about the lives of young women who worked in the meat processing plants. Contrasting the Victorian ideals of manners and gentility, the lives of the gut girls were bawdy and difficult. When a local Duchess undertakes to reform and refine the girls by training them at a club she sets up for them, their lives change immeasurably.

THE MONOLOGUE: Ellen (16 to 19) had been the most outspoken of the gut girls and had been trying to unite them into a Union. Unfortunately, before she could get them organized, the entire plant was closed down and they all lost their jobs. Not content to do what the Lady (Duchess) wanted, she tries to make ends meet her own way, and finds the going a lot harder than she anticipated.

TIME AND PLACE: Turn-of-the-century (1899–1900) England. Deptford. Ellen's room.

ELLEN: I pawned all my books today, but it doesn't matter. It wouldn't have mattered in the end what I'd said or done. It wouldn't have made a shred of difference what five hundred of us had done. We'd still have been out of work. They'd still have got their way — those people with their schemes and funds and clubs and allowances — all thought up out of fear — out of a fear that we, the ones who made their wealth might get out of hand. So we need to be tamed and trained to succumb to their values and orders. What's the point of kicking against it when all you damage is your foot. And I'm left trying to explain myself to, yes, even to Jasper and Sebastian who reply, "But Ellen, at least she found them all work." Yes, but in service — in service. I could tell by the look on their faces that they couldn't see anything wrong. Why should they? After all isn't that what we're here for? You service your husband and your children. What's wrong with servicing those deemed better than you — at least you get paid for it. I don't want to keep arguing and kicking against it. I don't want to stick out like a sore thumb and be seen as odd. Who am I to call the others fool, when I am the biggest laughing stock of the lot — actually believing that I had any say over what happened to me or anyone else. *(She tears the pawn ticket into pieces and throws it on the floor.)*

LOW LEVEL PANIC
by Clare McIntyre

Cockney British: Female

THE PLAY: A disturbing look into the lives of young, single, working women in present day London as they deal with feeling like prey for the men in the world, *Low Level Panic* is an intense, contemporary one-act with mature language and theme.

THE MONOLOGUE: Jo (20 to 22) describes her ideal self and her ideal evening to her roommate Mary.

TIME AND PLACE: Present. London. A flat (apartment) in a populated area of the city. Early evening. The bathroom of the flat (not the toilet, which is separate).

SPECIAL WORDS: Pissed means drunk; loo means toilet.

JO: If I could grow six inches and be as fat as I am now I'd be really tall and thin. I could stretch out all the fat on my legs till they were long and slender and I'd go to swanky bars and smoke menthol cigarettes and I'd wrap my new legs round cocktail stools and I'd smooth myself all over with my delicate hands and I'd have my hair up so you could see my neck. I'd save all the pennies I see lying about on the streets in an old whisky bottle then I'd go out and buy silky underwear with lots of lace on it and suspenders and that's what I'd wear. I wouldn't wear anything else because that would spoil it. I'd wear that and a lot of makeup and I'd snake my way around bars and hotels in Mayfair and I'd be able to drink whatever I like. I'd have cocktails and white wine out of bottles with special dates on them in tall glasses that were all dewy with cold and I'd smile a lot. I wouldn't laugh. I wouldn't guffaw. I'd just smile and show my teeth and I'd really be somebody then.

They'd see me approach. Just my feet in stilettos and the door would open like magic and uniformed men would be bowing. They wouldn't look at me: their eyes would be averted. I'd be able to get through doors without even turning the handles.

I wouldn't need anything. I wouldn't even have a bag. I'd have my lipstick on a chain round my neck. I'd play with my drink a bit, wiping the dewy bits off the glass and feeling my way up and down the stem with my fingers. Then I'd go to the loo and do my lipstick.

I'd meet someone. We'd just drink: play with our drinks and look at each other. We wouldn't really drink them. We wouldn't get pissed. We'd sit while the ice melted in them and they got all watery and we'd look at each other. He'd look at me, that is. I'd know he was looking at me and I'd look at myself in the mirror behind the bar. The whole place would be mirrors and he'd be looking at my legs . . . Then we'd leave. People would crash their cars when I got out in the street. There'd be cars jumping over each other to pick me up, men running towards me, desperate to get a closer look and try and touch me, touch my fur. But I wouldn't give anything away. I wouldn't get involved. I'd be wearing sunglasses, enormous, dark ones so they wouldn't see into me. I'd just be an amazing pair of legs, in sunglasses getting into a car.

THE MILL ON THE FLOSS
by George Eliot; adapted by Helen Edmundson

Standard British: Female

THE PLAY: Set in Victorian England, *The Mill on the Floss* is an adaptation of the famous novel of the same name. Using the device of actors playing multiple characters, and multiple actors playing *one* character, the story of family loyalty and love between rivals is brought to life. Maggie is played by three different actresses representing three distinct periods in her lifetime. As she grows up, and the events of her life propel her forward and force certain restrictions upon her, the Maggies of the past come into her consciousness and remind her of herself.

THE MONOLOGUE: Maggie (20s) has done an impetuous thing, she has left her fiancé and her family and has traveled downriver with a lover, Stephen. The further she gets from home, the more she realizes she cannot leave and tries to explain it to Stephen.

TIME AND PLACE: Victorian England. A small town near the Tewkesbury Mill on the River Avon (the Floss is a fictional river, but many think that Eliot was referring to the river near her home). Daytime.

MAGGIE: Stephen . . . Stephen, think how you felt about this two weeks ago. You felt that you owed yourself to another. So did I.

If life were quite easy and simple, as it might have been in paradise . . . I mean, if life did not make duties for us before love comes, then love would be a sign that two people belong together. But I know now that isn't true. There are things we must renounce in life; some of us must renounce love.

Do you think this is easy for me? I am only clinging to the one thing I can see clearly — that I must not, cannot seek my own happiness by sacrificing others. I would be haunted by the suffering I had caused. Our love would be poisoned. Don't you see? *(She starts to cry.)*

(Suddenly calm and brave.) There are things inside me you know nothing of. There are memories and affections and longings after perfect

goodness. They would never leave me for long. They would come back and be pain to me; repentance.

I have caused sorrow already. I know — I feel it. I will not cause more. It has never been my will to marry you. If I could wake back again into the time before this, I would choose to be true to my . . . to myself.

RELATIVELY SPEAKING
by Alan Ayckbourn

Standard British: Female

THE PLAY: A comedy of errors or double-entendre, this play is a "day in the life" of a young couple and the older couple they go to visit in the country. Greg is in love with Ginny. Ginny has had an affair with Philip. Philip and Sheila are married. On a normal day, Ginny convinces Greg that she is going to the country to visit her parents and that she must go alone. Greg, who has just proposed marriage to Ginny is not happy with that arrangement, so he sneaks aboard the train and attempts to surprise her at her "parents." When he arrives at Philip and Sheila's home, the comedy of misconstrued reality begins.

THE MONOLOGUE: Ginny (19 to 22) has come up to the country to end her relationship with Philip. He is unwilling to let her go so easily. She attempts to talk some sense into him.

TIME AND PLACE: Philip and Stella's country estate. Outside London. Later Sunday morning. Summer. Present.

GINNY: You'll let her go?

(Rising and turning upstage.) Don't you think if you went in there now, this minute, and told her about us, everything, she'd change her mind?

Isn't that really all she's waiting for? For you to tell her the truth?

Philip — be honest. Could you really do without her? *(Kneels by Philip's chair.)* Ask yourself, as you're sitting there now, full of the breakfast that she's cooked for you, sitting in the sunshine, waiting for the lunch that's bound to be coming — and the tea and the supper. And you know she'll have made the bed for you, not like me. You'll even get your glass of hot milk, I expect. And your clean shirt in the morning and your change of socks. They'll be waiting when you get up. And that's all Sheila. I bet she even cleans the bath out after you, doesn't she?

Then make it up with her. *(Rising.)* Before it's too late.

You must. Don't you see, Philip, you belong together — much more than we ever did. *(Philip nods and starts to move off — stands by gatepost.)*

ALMOST GROWN
by Richard Cameron

Cockney British: Male

THE PLAY: The events of childhood are revealed to have lasting impacts on three young men. We see their lives play out in their late teens as they take their separate paths, but we are also swept back to the days when they were careless schoolboys playing practical jokes on classmates. A tragic twist of fate brings the former friends face-to-face once more.

THE MONOLOGUE: Tommy (17) has run away from home and has landed at his older brother Eddie's house. Eddie wonders how Tommy got there, and Tommy, in a rambling thought, spills out all the reasons he's come to be where he is.

TIME AND PLACE: Present. Outskirts of London. Eddie's girlfriend's apartment.

TOMMY: The night I left she told me as far as she was concerned she had no children. I went mad. He come at me. I was smashing everything. I said I'd never go back. Never. She said she never wanted me back. Ever.

   I made up me mind I were gunna clear off, well out of it, well away, get as far away as I could. Go places, abroad and that. Travel the world, nick a bit, work a bit, scrounge my way around. But when I got to the end of our street, it started to hurt. Cuts, bruises. I thought he'd smashed me back in, and her. Thumping. It were killing. So I went to Dave Marshall's, stopped there the night. Thought I'd get off on my travels in the morning.

   I got delayed a bit.

   I was all set to go that day, made me mind up. Scott Carey came round. We all went down the river. I were thinking all the time, it's okay, when we're there I'll say "See you, I'm off" and I'll leave them, follow the river downstream. Down to the coast. Catch a ship, stow away, whatever.

   We met this girl we knew from school. Stella. She was with this new kid. Roberts. We were just messing about but she made it clear she fancied me, so we start a bit . . . He got the hump, so we stuck him down this hole, this old limekiln. The other two guard him, and me and her go off. She was all over me.

I told her what I was doing, running away. She wanted me to stay at her place. They had this big place, with all these outhouses. You can stay there, she says. And every night I'll bring you food and we'll do whatever you want. So I did. I went with her. Left Dave and Scott, and Roberts down the hole, and we just went off.

Stayed for about three weeks. Her dad was a doctor. Her Mam had a sports car. MG. They never knew I was there. I used to watch 'em come and go, went in the house when they'd gone. Massive house. Full of antiques. Guns and stuff. Her Mam had this head on her dressing table with a wig on it. Stella used to put it on and that. She got so . . . like she wanted to get caught. Got a kick out of it. She was weird. So I left. I didn't take anything. I could have done. Easy.

(Pause.)

EASY ACCESS (FOR THE BOYS)
by Claire Dowie

Cockney British: Male

THE PLAY: Told with the convention of a person being interviewed on videotape, the story centers on Michael, a young man who was molested by his father and has never actually dealt with the meaning of that event in his life. Now a hustler, he videotapes his diary in the hopes of gaining a better understanding of his world, his friends, his family and his feelings. Mature theme and language.

THE MONOLOGUE: In one of his "diary entries," Michael (18 to 20) addresses the audience and discusses his feelings about his new boyfriend, Matt. The relationship Matt has with his young daughter leaves Michael questioning the nature of a normal parent-child relationship and how it differed from his experience.

TIME AND PLACE: The present. South London.

MICHAEL: Matt I trust, I think. Well, sometimes I do. Sometimes I don't obviously. But basically I think I trust him more times than I don't so I suppose he's trustworthy. Basically. And I think Matt trusts me. He sort of accepts what I do, although we have the occasional argument about it but . . . I haven't told him about my dad, yet. I'm going to, I think it's necessary but . . . I suppose I'm waiting for the right time. No I'm not actually, to be honest I'm scared to death of telling him, I don't want to tell him. A lot of people, straight people, they go on about cycles of abuse and how abusers were once abused and . . . abuse breeding abuse breeding abuse and I wasn't abused, I know I wasn't abused but try telling that to people? Try telling them it's okay, no worries, I LIKE my dad. Try telling them I don't feel abused, I don't feel abusive, but then see how suspicious they become. So I don't know what he'd think and . . . I want him to want me. I like being with him. And little Becky. And he doesn't touch her at all, doesn't do anything, doesn't even cross his mind. I thought that was weird at first, I kept looking for signs, kept thinking oh he must be, why else would he want access? But he doesn't, he just loves her — normally. Had so much respect for him then. I suppose having Becky attracted me to him even more. Because I want to understand that, I want to be a part of something where sex isn't always at the heart of everything. Because to be honest I am so sick of sex, so . . . fed up with the cynicism of my friends and the pathetic maulings and maneuverings of punters. I'm getting old, getting too old for this game, I want something else.

EASY ACCESS (FOR THE BOYS)
by Claire Dowie

Cockney British: Male

THE PLAY: Told with the convention of a person being interviewed on videotape, the story centers on Michael, a young man who was molested by
his father and has never actually dealt with the meaning of that event in
his life. Now a hustler, he videotapes his diary in the hopes of gaining a
better understanding of his world, his friends, his family, and his feelings. Mature theme and language.

THE MONOLOGUE: Gary (18 to 20), Michael's best friend, was also abused by
his father when he was young. Also a hustler, Gary has a clearer and (he
thinks) healthier perspective on his abuse and abuser. He does a diary
entry for Michael's video and reveals his approach to life and people.

TIME AND PLACE: The present. South London.

GARY: I'm doing this because my friend Michael has asked me to. He wants
to be on telly, have fifteen minutes of fame. I think he's an arsehole, but,
because he's my friend I'm doing it. See, really, I couldn't give a toss what
people think. I have nothing in common with other people. As far as I'm
concerned other people are hypocrites or punters — or both. There's always an ulterior motive. Nobody does something for nothing. It's a
hobby with me now, trying to work out what someone wants. I'm getting quite good at it too, spotting the subtext. It's all power in one form
or another. One person trying to get power over another, trying to look
big by stepping on someone. Me and my friends we manipulate for
money, it's black and white, most people hate us for that. They hate us
because our ulterior motive is so clear, so blatant. They hate us because
we're honest, because we're not scurrying around trying to hide our ma-
nipulation, trying to cover up our power games. We're not tarting up our
greed and selfishness with pathetic words like love or friendship. My
friends are the only people I trust. My friends are honest. Of my friends
there is only one who wasn't abused as a child, and I think he's a liar. So
far as I'm concerned everybody else can go fuck themselves.

GREAT EXPECTATIONS
by Charles Dickens; adapted by John Clifford

Cockney British: Male

THE PLAY: In a dramatization of Dickens's famous novel, colorful and dramatic characters weave in and out of Pip's life in a rapid pace. True to the novel, Pip goes from extreme poverty to extreme wealth and back again in his quest for the truth about his life and the life of his love, Estella.

THE MONOLOGUE: Joe (late 20s to 30s) is Pip's dearest friend and his brother-in-law. Married to Pip's oldest sister, Joe has taken the young boy under his wing and is teaching him everything he can. His easy-going manner and approach to life and work is a comfort to the growing boy.

TIME AND PLACE: Victorian England. A small town in the countryside. Joe's iron-working forge. Daytime.

JOE: See here, Pip, my father he was given over to drink. And when he was overtook by drink, he hammered away at my mother most unmerciful. That was about the only hammering he ever did, Pip, when he weren't a-hammering at me. He was a blacksmith, too, see, Pip, right here in this forge.

Only he never hammered at the forge. He hammered at my mother instead. Consequence, Pip, my mother and me we ran away from home. And then my mother said, "Joe," she'd say, "now, Please God, you shall have some schooling," and she'd put me to school. But my father were that good in his heart that he couldn't bear to be without us. So he'd come along with the most tremenjous crowd and make such a row at the houses where we was that they used to have no more to do with us and give us up to him. And then he took us home and hammered us. And that, Pip, were a drawback on my learning.

But he was that good at heart he had no objection to my working, Pip. So I set to work and I kep him too, after a while.

Until he took a purple leptic fit and died.

And my mother followed soon after. She was in poor elth and quite broke. But she got her share of peace at last.

And then I was lonely, Pip. All alone out here on the forge. Out here on the edge of the lonesome marshes. And I met your sister.

And your sister, Pip, is a fine figure of a woman. A little sick and weak maybe, Pip, but a fine figure of a woman. You have to admit that. I mean, Pip, a little redness, or a little manner of bone, what does it signify?

Nothing at all, you're right, Pip. Right there. Nothing at all. And another thing. When I got acquainted with her, Pip, she had this miserable little creatur with her, and that were you, Pip.

But I did, Pip, I did. And when I offered your sister to keep company, I said, "Bring the poor little child," I said to her. "God bless the poor little child," I said, "there's room for him at the forge!"

And here we are, Pip. Ever the best of friends. Don't cry, old chap. Here we are. Ever the best of friends. Ain't us, Pip?

(They hug. Exit Joe.)

THE IMPORTANCE OF BEING EARNEST
by Oscar Wilde

Standard British: Male

THE PLAY: In this, one of Oscar Wilde's most famous plays, the lives of the hysterically superficial aristocracy are revealed for all their quirks and foibles. In the Victorian Era of manners and romance, Mr. Wilde pokes fun at the mores and constraints of the time in intelligent and surprising ways.

THE MONOLOGUE: John ("Earnest") Worthing (29) has proposed to the honorable Gwendolyn Fairfax, Algernon Moncrief's cousin, but her mother, Lady Bracknell, does not approve of the pairing. When Algernon learns of Jack's adorable young ward, Cecily, he visits Jack's country house and wins her affections by pretending to be Jack's fictional brother, "Earnest." When Algernon's aunt appears and learns of her nephew's plan to marry the young woman, Jack steps in and informs her of *his* objections to the pairing.

TIME AND PLACE: London, England. 1800s. Jack Worthing's country estate.

JACK: I beg your pardon for interrupting you, Lady Bracknell, but this engagement is quite out of the question. I am Miss Cardew's guardian, and she cannot marry without my consent until she comes of age. That consent I absolutely decline to you.

[LADY BRACKNELL: Upon what grounds, may I ask? Algernon is an extremely, I may almost say an ostentatiously, eligible young man. He has nothing, but he looks everything. What more can one desire?]

JACK: It pains me very much to have to speak frankly to you, Lady Bracknell, about your nephew, but the fact is that I do not approve at all of his moral character. I suspect him of being untruthful.

(Algernon and Cecily look at him in indignant amazement.)

[LADY BRACKNELL: Untruthful! My nephew Algernon? Impossible! He is an Oxonian.]

JACK: I fear there can be no possible doubt about the matter. This afternoon during my temporary absence in London on an important question of romance, he obtained admission to my house by means of the false pretense of being my brother. Under an assumed name he drank, I've just been informed by my butler, an entire pint bottle of my Perrier-Jouet, Brut, '89; wine I was specially reserving for myself. Continuing his disgraceful deception, he succeeded in the course of the afternoon in alienating the affections of my only ward. He subsequently stayed to tea, and devoured every single muffin. And what makes his conduct all the more heartless is, that he was perfectly aware from the first that I have no brother, that I never had a brother, and that I don't intend to have a brother, not even of any kind. I distinctly told him so myself yesterday afternoon.

OURSELVES ALONE
by Anne Devlin

Standard British: Male

THE PLAY: Set in Northern Ireland, the complicated and intrigue-filled lives of a Republican family are given full view as the individuals plot, scheme, betray, and love amidst the constant threat of being found out by British intelligence.

THE MONOLOGUE: Joe (20s) is a British expatriate offering his services to the revolutionary forces in Northern Ireland. He must endure an interrogation to determine whether or not he is actually some sort of double agent attempting to steal into the confidence of the revolutionaries only to then expose them to the British police. Joe's impassioned response to the lengthy interrogation convinces his questioners to believe in his sincerity.

TIME AND PLACE: A back room in West Belfast, Northern Ireland. Present. Summer. Evening.

JOE: It's not true. She was never happy about going there. She hated it. And I did too. But — I gave her no choice. She even used to cry a lot before she went. And then she'd get there and start talking to Alice. It was like a flood. The sun came out. I never knew how she did it. And because she cheered up, I thought she didn't mind in the end. I really believed everything was all right. I have not been recruited by British Intelligence. They never approached me; in fact it's been quite the opposite since I bought myself out of the Army. I met Rosa, as you know, while I was at university in Dublin. My family never approved of my going back to Ireland. My mother saw it as a rejection of her in going there and leaving the Army as I did. She actually complained once to my sister that I married Rosa to spite her, to make her ashamed. A wee hussy from the Bogside, she called her. In marrying Rosa I was also a security risk. My sister even suggested to me that her husband would probably never be made a colonel because of my connections with the wrong side in the Irish War. Not one member of my family came to the wedding. The Army of course refused permission to the Blakemores to attend, something to do with Rosa's part in the Bogside Riots of sixty-nine. She was a member of the Citizens' Defense Committee and her name was on the list of conditions which she handed to the Army on their arrival in Derry prior to dismantling the barricades. One of the conditions was a general amnesty for all those people defending their homes in the barricaded area. The barricades came down. However the Army Council and Blakemore's superiors still regarded my wife as a rioter. *(Pause.)* There is one thing you should know. Eighteen months ago at Sandhurst, I did try to meet Kitson. I asked Blakemore to arrange a meeting for me. I had very selfish reasons for doing so. I wanted to interview him for a paper I was giving at a conference in Stockholm on Insecurity and the State. It would have been a great coup. When I suggested a drink with Kitson either at the mess or at the house, Blakemore refused point blank. My brother-in-law doesn't like him — Kitson has no small talk. My family has nothing but. *(Pause.)* When Rosa left me, she said she regarded all her association with me as a betrayal of her tribe. I really didn't know what she meant at the time. I was deeply mortified and ashamed. Because I do believe she was happy with me once. *(A long pause. Then Josie comes back to the table.)*

RELATIVELY SPEAKING
by Alan Ayckbourn

Standard British: Male

THE PLAY: A comedy of errors or double-entendre, this play is a "day in the life" of a young couple and the older couple they go to visit in the country. Greg is in love with Ginny. Ginny has had an affair with Philip. Philip and Sheila are married. On a normal day, Ginny convinces Greg that she is going to the country to visit her parents and that she must go alone. Greg, who has just proposed marriage to Ginny is not happy with that arrangement, so he sneaks aboard the train and attempts to surprise her at her "parents." When he arrives at Philip and Sheila's home, the comedy of misconstrued reality begins.

THE MONOLOGUE: Greg (19 to 22) woke up suspicious. As Ginny prepared to leave, he attempts to explain away his sense that something is not quite right.

TIME AND PLACE: Ginny's flat. Sunday morning. Summer. Present.

GREG: *(Rising and wandering downstage right and then slowly up towards her.)* It was rather odd really. When I got up just now I was a bit dozy, you know, and I did what I do at home — I fished with my feet under the bed for my slippers. One of my habits, that is, one of my idiosyncrasies — it helps me to recognize myself when I'm half asleep. I always think that's important, don't you? That the first thing you do when you wake up in the morning is to make sure you know who you are. I have a terror of that, losing my identity in the night. Some people are frightened of burglars breaking in. With me, it's stealthy midnight brainwashers. *(Sitting beside her on the bed.)* Anyway, I did this fishing with my feet business, and I thought to myself, steady lad, you're in for a shock. They won't be there. This is her flat you're in. Don't panic now. You're the same person you were when you went to sleep. Only the bed has been changed. And then, the blow. A pair of alien slippers attached themselves to my toes. I can tell you that was an experience I wouldn't care to go through again. It could have split my personality right up the middle. Did you know that? Very nasty.

RELATIVELY SPEAKING
by Alan Ayckbourn

Standard British: Male

THE PLAY: A comedy of errors or double-entendre, this play is a "day in the life" of a young couple and the older couple they go to visit in the country. Greg is in love with Ginny. Ginny has had an affair with Philip. Philip and Sheila are married. On a normal day, Ginny convinces Greg that she is going to the country to visit her parents and that she must go alone. Greg, who has just proposed marriage to Ginny is not happy with that arrangement, so he sneaks aboard the train and attempts to surprise her at her "parents." When he arrives at Philip and Sheila's home, the comedy of misconstrued reality begins.

THE MONOLOGUE: Greg (19 to 22) has just intruded on the lives of Sheila and Philip, Ginny's "parents." He has been trying to forge a bond with Sheila to eventually ask her permission to marry Ginny.

TIME AND PLACE: Philip and Sheila's country estate. Later Sunday morning. Summer. Present.

GREG: That's all right. Probably me. I get nervous at meeting new people. Not just you. Everybody. Even bus conductors. You know, there's some mornings, I get on a bus and, I don't know if you feel the same, but I'm sitting there and there he is, the conductor, working his way down the bus towards me, and I think to myself, this morning I'm not going to be able to speak to this bloke. Not a word. He's going to say: Where to, mate? And I'm going to open my mouth and go huuuhh . . . open my mouth and nothing comes out. So when I feel like this, I have to practice, you see. I sit there, saying it over to myself . . . four-penny one . . . One morning I was doing this, I was rehearsing everything, even rehearsing the good morning I was going to say to my landlady . . . and I got on the bus and asked for ten cigarettes. I couldn't speak for the rest of the day after that.

ROSENCRANTZ AND GUILDENSTERN ARE DEAD
by Tom Stoppard

Standard or Cockney British: Males

THE PLAY: The brilliant Mr. Stoppard gives us a witty, behind-the-scenes look into the lives of Hamlet's friends, Rosencrantz and Guildenstern, before and after they meet up with Hamlet at Elsinore.

THE MONOLOGUE: While waiting to meet up with Hamlet, Rosencrantz (20 to 22) and Guildenstern pass the time engaging in deep, philosophical conversations.

TIME AND PLACE: Two Elizabethans passing the time in a place without any visible character.

NOTE: The pacing of the piece should include the pauses that are both written and in the punctuation (ellipses, etc.).

ROSENCRANTZ: *(Pause.)* Do you ever think of yourself as actually *dead,* lying in a box with a lid on it?
  Nor do I, really . . . It's silly to be depressed by it. I mean one thinks of it like being *alive* in a box, one keeps forgetting to take into account the fact that one is *dead* . . . which should make all the difference . . . shouldn't it? I mean, you'd never *know* you were in a box, would you? It would be just like being *asleep* in a box. Not that I'd like to sleep in a box, mind you, not without any air — you'd wake up dead, for a start, and then where would you be? Apart from inside a box. That's the bit I don't like, frankly. That's why I don't think of it . . .
(Guildenstern stirs restlessly, pulling his cloak round him.)
Because you'd be helpless, wouldn't you? Stuffed in a box like that, I mean You'd be in there for ever. Even taking into account the fact that you're dead, it isn't a pleasant thought. *Especially* if you're dead, really . . . *ask* yourself, if I asked you straight off — I'm going to stuff you in this box now, would you rather be alive or dead? Naturally, you'd prefer to be alive. Life in a box is better than no life at all. I expect. You'd have a chance at least. You could lie there thinking — well, at least I'm not

dead! In a minute someone's going to bang on the lid and tell me to come out. *(Banging on the floor with his fists.)* "Hey you, whatsyername! Come out of there!"

(Pause.)

I wouldn't think about it, if I were you. You'd only get depressed. *(Pause.)* Eternity is a terrible thought. I mean, where's it going to end?

QUARTERMAINE'S TERMS
by Simon Gray

Standard British: Male

THE PLAY: Set in a private school in England which serves primarily foreign
students, *Quartermaine's Terms* gives us a behind-the-scenes look at the
faculty of such a school and the trials and tribulations that beset them.
Centered around the aging star teacher, Quartermaine, the play reveals
the complex dramas in the lives of five other teachers . . . and as time
passes, the journey of each individual character is shown to be in stark
contrast to where they began.

THE MONOLOGUE: Derek Meadle (20 to 22) has been teaching at the school
for a year now and still hasn't become "permanent" (privy to holiday
benefits and pay). The work load and the impending pressure of taking
care of a family has begun to wear out Derek's usually mild manner. He
attempts, kindly, to get what he needs from Henry (his boss), and his intentions continue to fall just slightly short of being understood.

TIME AND PLACE: The Cull-Loomis School of English for Foreigners. Cambridge, England. Early 1960s. At the start of the day.

NOTE: St. John is pronounced "Sin Jn" in England.

MEADLE: Ah yes, Henry, but you see I don't get paid during vacations, you
see. I only get paid by the hour for the hours I'm allowed to do, while
the rest of the staff get paid an annual salary. So even though I'm cur-
rently doing twice as many hours again as — well, St. John for example,
I in fact get slightly less than half of what St. John gets, over the year. I
mean, take this half-term we've just had, Henry, a week of paid holiday
for everybody else but a week of no money at all for me, it was just luck
that my aunt died in it, or I might have had to miss an earning week to
go to her funeral and sort out my uncle you see. — And last Christmas,
well, I've kept this very quiet, Henry, but last Christmas I had to be a
postman. *(He laughs.)*
     Yes, and let me tell you it wasn't simply the work, Henry — being
up at six, and trudging through the snow and sleet we had the whole of

those three weeks — it was also the sheer embarrassment. Twice during my second round I nearly bumped into some students. I only got away with it because I kept my head lowered and once Thomas himself went right past me in the car — it was a miracle he didn't see me, especially as I'd slipped on some ice and I was actually lying on the pavement with the letters scattered everywhere — and now the summer holiday's looming ahead — I simply don't know how I'm going to get through that. Or at least I do. I've already sent in my application to be an Entertainments Officers at a holiday camp in Cleethorpes.

(Laughing.) But that's life, isn't it? That's the joke. How hard I've worked. I mean, old Quartermaine here — well, according to one of the Swedes I'm not allowed to mention because it's a fraction on the unethical side to speak ill of a colleague — well, he sometimes sits for a whole hour not speaking. Even in dictation classes or if he does condescend to speak, goes off into little stories about himself they can't make head or tail of.

QUARTERMAINE'S TERMS
by Simon Gray

Standard British: Male

THE PLAY: Set in a private school in England which serves primarily foreign students, *Quartermaine's Terms* gives us a behind-the-scenes look at the faculty of such a school and the trials and tribulations that beset them. Centered around the aging star teacher, Quartermaine, the play reveals the complex dramas in the lives of five other teachers . . . and as time passes, the journey of each individual character is shown to be in stark contrast to where they began.

THE MONOLOGUE: Derek Meadle (20 to 22) has been teaching at the school for a year now and still hasn't become "permanent" (privy to holiday benefits and pay). The work load and the impending pressure of taking care of a family has begun to wear out Derek's usually mild manner. After making no progress in his attempt to become permanent and to receive a raise, his emotions have got the better of him and he loses his cool while trying to explain his belief in his worthiness.

TIME AND PLACE: The Cull-Loomis School of English for Foreigners. Cambridge, England. Early 1960s. At the start of the day.

MEADLE: *(There is a pause.)* Oh, what does it matter? Everybody knows that for you one Swede is like another German, one Greek is like another Italian, you can't tell them apart and you don't know what they're called — unlike me, you see — because do you know what I do? I memorize their names before their first class, and then study their faces during it, and then when I go home I close my eyes and practice putting the two together so that by the second class I know every one of my students *personally,* and do you know what else I do, I keep a lookout not only in term time but also in my holidays — my *unpaid* holidays — for any item that might interest them for British Life and Institutions and actually make a note of them — here — in my notebook, which I always keep especially in my pocket *(Wrestling with it with increasing violence, jerking it out of his pocket, tearing his pocket as he does so.)* along with any of the out-of-the-way idioms and interesting usages I might happen across — and do you know what *else* I do — I — but what does it matter what else I do, that's what I mean by joke of life or whatever it is, because I'm the one that's facing the push, and you're the one that's on Permanent. *(During this speech, Meadle's accent has become increasingly North Country.)* Not that I begrudge you — it's just that I reckon that I've earned it. Look — look, I don't mean — I don't mean — the last thing I mean is — *(He turns away, possibly in tears.)*

(There is silence, into which Melanie enters, through the French windows.)

SECTION TWO

IRISH

Irish Introduction

With its enchanting musical inflection and the colloquial use of colorful expressions, it is no wonder that the Irish dialect is one of the most popular dialects in today's theater scene. Indeed, with the abundance of Irish works being staged all over America, many actors are hurrying to the nearest dialect coach to develop an Irish accent. Not only can the dialect be heard on many American stages, but it can also be found in many popular films in our video stores and movie theaters.

Just as there are many dialect variations of Standard British, there are many dialect variations of Irish. Northern Ireland, a separate nation, has a distinctly different dialect than its near neighbor, Northwest Ireland. The West Ireland dialect (namely Galway) differs greatly from the more metropolitan (lighter) dialect of Dublin (located in Eastern Ireland). Then there's County Cork, thought by some to contain the most lyrical and "traditional" of the Irish dialects. What Americans tend to do when they fake an Irish accent is a bad version of County Cork sounds.

For our purposes, we will apply some general, consistent sound changes that should give you a general, mostly West Ireland–sounding dialect.

The Irish dialect can trace its roots to the original speakers of the Celtic language — the Pagans who originally inhabited Ireland. Because their religious rituals were not written down, they passed on their traditions and stories by singing. As the language evolved, and the social structure of Ireland evolved (due to the conquering peoples which took over the land), the dialect evolved into a singing version of English.

The music of the Irish dialect is key to its reproduction, but it can become too singsong if you are not careful. Always remember the point of the sentence, not the notes.

The Irish people are warm, hospitable, and generous, and they are masters at conversation. Their speech is filled with proverbs, metaphors, clichés and quotations from plays, songs, or films. There is a joy in speaking that comes through in the delivery. This is not to say that there are no sad people in Ireland; indeed, there is always a sense of deep-seated sorrow at the core of the Irish, but this sorrow is masked in the twinkling of the "Irish eyes."

As with any dialect, you must first know your character's life circumstances to accurately reproduce his or her speech patterns. With the Irish, this is important to avoid overgeneralizing your approach to the material and playing simply a singsong action on your lines. Subtler is better with the Irish dialect.

- When telling a story or personal anecdote, the music of the Irish dialect is more present than when simply speaking a normal sentence. For example, if you were to tell your parents about an incident that happened to you at school that really affected you, your voice would become more animated and energized. The same is true for the strength of the Irish dialect. When they are narrating a story, they color it with all the vocal colors they can. The music plays in their voices.

- Due perhaps in part to the origins of the Irish culture (Celtic, Pagan tribes), and the exceedingly harsh conditions (cold, rural, isolated, semi-barren land) in which they have lived over the past hundreds of years, the Irish have a tendency to be a spiritual people. Although the dominant religion at this time is Catholicism, the Irish have been known to believe in (or tell stories about) things that are of a more fantastical or imaginary nature (i.e., fairies, banshees, and leprechauns). Historically, the Irish needed to explain their tragedies away, and belief in the supernatural sometimes seemed the only comfort.

- The Irish dialect is musical. The music comes from extending the length of the vowel sounds and moving the pitch/note of the sound up and down.

- Again, due to environmental conditions (cold, fog, wind) there is a lack of mouth opening and movement when the Irish produce sounds.

- Because the Irish use so many quotations, proverbs, and clichés in their everyday speech, they tend to speak faster than the average person. They compose their thoughts quickly and with the skill of old, professional orators.

- When the Irish *do* pause to compose a thought, the nonverbal interjection they use instead of our American *um* is *am*.

- More noticeably than with the English accents, the Irish have colloquialisms that are more rhythmic in their literature. Usually these phrases, words or interjections are not to be taken literally but poetically as part of the natural rhythm of the line.

- The Irish do a few vowel sounds with a sense of tightening and closing of the lips. These sounds are traditionally diphthongs (two vowel sounds made in the time of one), but they make only the first sound of the diphthong and hold it for a longer time. To master these sounds, you must first observe what your mouth does when it makes these sounds normally. It is called "Irish lengthening" in the section that follows.

Irish Film, Television, and Audio References

FILMS

Rural West Ireland:
Riders to the Sea
The Butcher Boy
Waking Ned Devine
Angela's Ashes

Rural North Ireland (Donegal):
Dancing at Lughnasa
The Field
The Secret of Roan Inish
The Closer You Get

North Ireland (Belfast):
Michael Collins
In the Name of the Father
The Crying Game
Titanic Town

South Ireland (Dublin):
My Left Foot
The Commitments
Circle of Friends

Americanized Irish (actors doing Irish accents):
The Brothers McMullen
Far and Away

TELEVISION
PBS Special: "The Irish in America"

DIALECT TAPES AND SOURCES
Irish   Gillian Lane-Plescia
Stage Dialects and More Stage Dialects   Jerry Blunt
Dialects for the Stage   Evangeline Machlin
Acting with an Accent — Irish   David Alan Stern
IDEA website   www.ukans.edu/~idea/index.html

For a more complete and detailed list of films/resources, see Ginny Kopf's book The
Dialect Handbook.

Irish Elements and Sounds

- The *r* of the Irish: Unlike the Standard British dialect, the Irish produce what we call a hard *r*. The hard *r* sound is produced with the tongue arching up toward gum ridge behind the top teeth. The *r* is not trilled like the Scots, but just pronounced.

- The Irish lengthening: When producing these sounds, always make sure that your voice stays supported and well placed, otherwise the tension may cause some vocal exhaustion.

  [oh] → [o:] don't, go, show, slow, road → do:n't, go:, sho:, slo:, ro:d (round your lips to make the [oh] sound and then keep them there, don't let them move as you say [o:] out loud. Add some time to it and hold the sound now.)

  [ay] → [eh] take, name, face, Kate, plate → te:k, ne:m, fe:s, Ke:t, ple:t (smile and prepare to make the [ay] sound but keep your mouth in position and lengthen the first half of the sound only.)

- Other Irish vowel/consonant changes:

  [ih] → [eh] hill, different, dig, quick, thick → hehll, dehfrent, dehg, quehck, thehck

  [uh] → [u] (the schwa sound becomes more like the [u] sound as in the word "put" or "took") mother, from, love, button, won → muther, frum, luv, buttn, wun

  [th] → [t] thirty, cathedrals, thanked, theater → tairty, catedrals, tanked, teater

  [th] → [dh] this, them, those, weather → dhis, dhem, dhose, weadher

  [ing] → [in] drop the *g* on -ing endings

  [er/ir] → [air] girl, heard, bird → gairl, haird, baird

[or] → [are] word, storm, forth → ward, starm, farth

[ow] → [uh-oo] now, town, without → nuh-oo, tuh-oon, wit uh-oot

[oy] → [y] boy, joy, noise, toys → by, jy, nyz, tyz
(occasional change)

[y] → [oy] Ireland, my, kite → oyrland, moy, koyt
(occasional change)

[t]/[d] → [t(h)/d(h)] better, door, drink, what, write → bet(h)er, d(h)oor, d(h)rink, what(h), wroyt(h)
The consonant [t] and [d] sounds are dentalized (meaning your tongue is touching the back of your top teeth) and lots of air falls off those sounds. In some Irish plays, this element of the dialect is spelled out in the script writing by adding an [h] after the [t] or [d] (i.e., "better" would be written "betther"). Just think of the [h] symbol as a clue to have a bit more air come out after you make the consonant sound.

[a] becomes not as crisp as the Pure Anne sound. Round your lips and say "ah" and then smile to make this sound in the words like "grand," "Pat," "and," etc. Another way to think of this sound is to imagine the American Southern way of saying "I."
Words: grand, fan, pat, wrap, flat, cat, Anne, Adam, stand, ran, land

IRISH PRACTICE SENTENCES

[r]

> Here where their car started the yard parted. Park your car and start your heart.

[o:]

> Go slow near the show by the road, Joe. The crow ate the doe.

[e:]

> You can take me name but you can't take me face. Stay Kate, stay and play with Kay.

[ih] → [eh]

> The hills look different when you dig. Quick, pick up the stick, ya thick!

[uh] → [u]

> Me mother loves me brother more. I won a button from London.

[th] → [t]

> The thirty cathedrals thought the theater was through. Thanks for the oath of thinking.

[ing] → [in]

> The crying working man was drinking and thinking about skiing.

[er/ir] → [air]

> The first bird is early and dirty.

[or] → [are]

> Work is the worst when it hurts.

[ow] → [uh-oo]

> Now the sound of the round crowd fills the town. The crown fell down on the ground.

[oy] → [y]

Me boy's toys make a load of noise. The joy is noisy in the Toy Shoppe.

[y] → [oy]

Ireland is the right bright light. At night the sky is ripe with flying spies.

[t/d] → [t(h)/d(h)]

You'd better not drink that water. Don't drink drunk. Take that tired talk home.

A LITTLE LIKE PARADISE
by Niall Williams

Irish: Female

THE PLAY: Set in a rural seaside village in County Clare, *A Little Like Paradise* describes both the impression the town has on its old inhabitants and the miraculous events that occur within the play. A near-death in the local pub makes the place a shrine for the devout as the politics, loves, and lives of the townsfolk intersect all at once inside its walls.

THE MONOLOGUE: Mary (20) misses her husband, Francis. He went off to America to find his fortune and was supposed to write and call more often. She reveals to a friend her and Francis's plan for their new lives in America.

TIME AND PLACE: 1992. Outside near the beach. Caherconn, County Clare, Ireland. Near evening.

MARY: Did you ever sit down and think of all the things you thought about somebody and never said to them?

Never said you know I really admire the way you did this or that. There's something about the way you walk or talk or the way you say my name or . . .

Silly things. I like your handwriting. I keep bits of it in my purse, envelopes, anything. Or I'm still buying the cornflakes you liked and you're not even here. I let the toothpaste be squeezed from the middle now and I'm sorry I ever made a fuss about it; of course you have to get dirt in the house getting turf in, ashes do go everywhere, and you always said, and I disagreed, God and I was stupid to keep bringing it up and I should have said so, and I should have said you know I love that red jumper on you and you're really great you know, you lighten up the place, oh hundreds and hundreds of other things, every day , and oh God I didn't and now I don't know . . .

He's not coming home . . .

No, he's not. He told his father that he was, that he was only going out to make the money for the house and come home, because he couldn't bring himself to tell him. Not then anyway, not when he was going.

You know what Mr. McInerney's like. And well, Francie's supposed to just get things set up out there and then I'm coming out to him.

We're going to live in San Francisco. I have the visa got and everything, and now he hasn't written to me, and he's out there, you know, out there, and I'm thinking maybe he's changed his mind and met someone and doesn't . . . well maybe he's remembering the way I was on at him, they were stupid, stupid things — God, Mary, you're such an eejit, you are such an eejit — telling him how to fold his shirts and he packing, asking him how much, well how much do you love me, Francie, go on, tell me, and he all knotted up in himself with his father downstairs fuming and he firing the things in the case and enough Mary he says enough and I said, well fine, well fine for you Francie McInerney excuse me for asking but that's not enough for me. I charged out of the place and he didn't come after me like he always does, he didn't come after me at all. And then the next morning going to Shannon in the car he hardly said a word either, just sitting there watching us leaving Caherconn out by Shaghnessy's and the Heihir's old place where he told me he used to help with the baling, and all the time nothing, not a peep out of him up in the front next to his father, neither of them cracking a word between them, and me, oh I was lovely bawling my eyes out like a right eejit at the bottom of the crying stairs. The last I saw of him *(Pause.)* And then he was gone.

Well so, anyway I have this book and it says, you know, you could do it, go out on your soul sort of, communicate in spirits, and so I was thinking maybe I could, like Mr. Maguire, and maybe I know, I know it sounds crazy but I could sort of get on to Francie you know, sort of let him know and that I loved him. What do you think?

THE LOVERS
by Brian Friel

Irish: Female

THE PLAY: Surprising and tragic, Brian Friel's look at the lives of two young lovers seems innocent enough, and then takes a surprising twist. Told in two parts, in the first section of the play, the action is taken by the young lovers as we hear the narration of the older lovers. The narration takes an "evening news broadcast" tone which starkly contrasts the vibrancy and life of the lovers we watch. The tone proves to be effective in the set-up of the eventual tragedy. The second half of the play reverses the roles as the young lovers become the narrators of the older lovers' story.

THE MONOLOGUE: On a beautiful early summer afternoon, Joe and Mag (both 17) meet to study for their (GED) tests. Maggie, expecting Joe's baby soon, cannot seem to keep her thoughts on her books.

TIME AND PLACE: A hilltop in Ballymore (a fictional town). County Donegal. Ireland. Late afternoon. June 1966.

Mag is drowsy with the heat. Her head is propped against her case. Through slitted eyes she surveys the scene below in Ballymore. She is addressing Joe but knows that he is not listening to her.

MAG: I can see the boarders out on the tennis courts. They should be studying. And there's a funeral going up High Street; nine cars and a petrol lorry, and an ambulance. Maybe the deceased was run over by the petrol lorry — the father of a large family — and the driver is paying his respects and crying his eyes out. If he doesn't stop blubbering, he'll run over someone else. And the widow is in the ambulance, all in plaster, crippled for life. *(She tries out a mime of this — both arms and legs cast in awkward shapes.)* And the children are going to be farmed out to cruel aunts with squints and mustaches. Sister Michael has a beard. Joan O'Hara says she shaves with a cutthroat every first Friday and uses an after-shave lotion called Virility. God, nuns are screams if you don't take them seriously. I think I'd rather be a widow than a widower; but I'd rather be a bachelor than a spinster. And I'd rather be deaf than dumb; but I'd rather be dumb than blind. And if I had to choose between lung cancer, a coronary, and multiple sclerosis, I'd take the coronary. Papa's family all died of coronaries, long before they were commonplace. *(She sits up to tell the following piece of family history.)* He had a sister, Nan, who used to sing at the parochial concert every Christmas; and one year, when she was singing *Jerusalem* — you know, just before the chorus, when the piano is panting Huh-huh-huh-huh-huh-huh, she opened her mouth and dropped like a log . . .

Joe, d'you think *(Quoting something she has read.)* my legs have got thick, my body gross, my facial expression passive to dull, and my eyes lack-luster? I hope it's a boy, and that it'll be like you — with a great big bursting brain. Or maybe it'll be twins — like me. I wonder what Peter would have been like? Sometimes when she's very ill Mother calls me Peter. If it were going to be twins I'd rather have a boy and a girl than two boys or two girls; but if it were going to be triplets I'd rather have two boys and a girl or two girls and a boy than three boys or three girls. *(Very wisely and directed to Joe.)* And I have a feeling it's going to be premature.

Mothers have intuitions about these things. We were premature. Five weeks. Very tricky.

THE LOVERS
by Brian Friel

Irish: Female

THE PLAY: Surprising and tragic, Brian Friel's look at the lives of two young lovers seems innocent enough, and then takes a surprising twist. Told in two parts, in the first section of the play, the action is taken by the young lovers as we hear the narration of the older lovers. The narration takes an "evening news broadcast" tone which starkly contrasts the vibrancy and life of the lovers we watch. The tone proves to be effective in the set-up of the eventual tragedy. The second half of the play reverses the roles as the young lovers become the narrators of the older lovers' story.

THE MONOLOGUE: On a beautiful early summer afternoon, Joe and Mag (both 17) meet to study for their (GED) tests. Maggie, expecting Joe's baby soon, cannot seem to keep her thoughts on her books. Even though Joe seems not to be listening, she cannot help but continue to chatter away on this beautiful Ballymore day.

TIME AND PLACE: A hilltop in Ballymore (a fictional town). County Donegal. Ireland. Late afternoon. June 1966.

Mag has another twinge of conscience: she plunges into her book again.

MAG: *(Reads.)* LP, MQ, and NR are ordinates perpendicular to the axis OX such that LP = 8", MQ = 7", and NR = 4". Find the lengths of ordinates at the midpoints of LM and MN of the circular arc through P, Q, and R, and by means of Simpson's rule and the five ordinates estimate . . . *(Her concentration fails.)* Everything's so still. That's what I love. At a time like this, if I close my eyes and scarcely breathe, I sometimes have very important philosophic thoughts — about existence and life and et cetera. That's what people mean when they talk of a woman's intuitions. Every woman has intuitions but I think that pregnant women have more important intuitions than non-pregnant women. And another thing too: a woman's intuitions are more important while she's pregnant than after she's had her baby. So when you see a pregnant woman sitting at the fire, knitting, not talking, you can be sure she's having very important philosophic thoughts about things. I wish to God I could knit. Years and years ago in primary school I began a pair of gloves; but the fingers scootrified me and I turned them into ankle socks . . .

I think your father's a highly intellectual man, really; a born naturalist. And your mother — she's so practical and so unassuming. That's what I want to be. One of these days I'm going to stop talking altogether — for good — and people will say: Didn't Mrs. Joseph Brennan become dignified all of a sudden? Since the baby arrived, I suppose. I think now, Joe, it's going to be nineteen days overdue. And in desperation they'll bring me into the hospital and put me on the treadmill — that's a new yoke they have to bring on labor; Joan told me about it. An aunt of a second cousin of hers was on it non-stop for thirteen hours. They keep you climbing up this big wheel that keeps giving away under you. Just like the slaves in olden times. And after the baby's born they'll keep it in an oxygen tent for a fortnight. And when we get it home it'll have to be fed with an eye dropper every forty-nine minutes and we'll get no sleep at all and — *(Sudden alarming thought.)* My God, you won't get asthma like your father when you get old, will you?

OUR LADY OF SLIGO
by Sebastian Barry

Irish: Female

THE PLAY: With a series of flashbacks and monologues, the story of the demise of Mai O'Hara is told. Dying of liver cancer in the Jervis Street Hospital, Mai's life flashes before her eyes. Her husband Jack and their daughter Joanie visit them both in the present time and in her memory. Haunted by the loss of her infant son, the deeds of her drunken past, and the love of her father, Mai comes to terms with her choices and sets her sights to the end of the journey.

THE MONOLOGUE: Joanie (20) visits her mom and tries to get some closure on the issues that plague her life . . . issues brought to her by the behavior of her parents during her childhood. Mai, in a semi-aware state, is still able to convey a sense of sorrow and apology to Joanie.

TIME AND PLACE: Mai's hospital room at the Jervis Street Hospital. Early evening. 1950s. Dublin.

SPECIAL IRISH PRONUNCIATIONS IN THIS MONOLOGUE:
feisanna = fesh uh nuh (an Irish dance)
"Baidin Fheilimi" = bah jean (little boat) eye luh mee (a town)
Nil aon tintean mar do thinteain fein = neel ayn tintawn mahr duh
   hintawn fayn
Knocknarea = nok nuh ray
Maeve = mave
Cairn = kairn

JOANIE: Mammy, he pulled me from sleep every night of my life, sometimes I was already half-awake, listening to the voices in the bedroom above, going on like those bitter waves shuffling the dark shingle at Strandhill. And the gramophone going throughout. Nothing stopped the gramophone, Yma Sumac and her eight octaves, Hoagy Carmichael down in Old Hong Kong. Daddy pulled me from sleep like he might drag up a full bucket from the deepest well, his fatherly arms pulling hand over hand and the water of dreams and fear spilling darkly into the receding pit. I sang for you both through a *feisanna* to stop those voices, to stop him coming in to waken me, I was willing to sing the hardest song in dark Irish, with the trickiest twiddly bits on the piano between verses. And I stood on the stages of Sligo, Roscommon and Galway, singing *"Báidín Fheilimi"* and "She Moved through the Fair" and sang out clear and strong in the hope that your bickering and warring would stop.

I sang so that the stinking glasses would not be there one morning, perched on the turn of the banisters, or fallen over the parlour, the little mole-heaps of cigarettes in the stabbed ashtrays. Every morning was solemn as a battlefield with the sad corpses of bottles killed on the scummy carpets and I was like a general sad in the aftermath. All the singing in the world couldn't stop it, though I might burst my breastbone in the singing. *Nil aon tinteán mar do thinteáin féin,* said the teacher, there's no hearth like your own hearth, but she wanted to know why my eyes were black from lack of sleep and when I fell asleep in the hot class-room she was constrained to beat me, bound by the laws governing the mysteries of children to beat me.

Mammy, why did you fold me up in the filthy blankets of the small hours, why did Daddy come in and wake me and send me up the stairs to your bed, him getting into my own warm nest, me just a shard of hu-manity walking up through the salty moonlight, and the terrible yawp of the attic stairs beyond where the hag of Beare sat in the sucking shadow? And the whale in the bed that was my Mammy, snoring like a man, and those extraordinary farts you made in the cowl of smeared sheets . . .

. . . and me slipping in beside you like a salmon into a ruined river. And breathing then with hardship I was, a little engine of distress. And I used to think of the warrior asleep in his stone hut on Knocknarea at the foot of Maeve's gigantic cairn, guarding his queen eternally, and I won-dered, was I doing the same? Did every broken mother need a sheltering child? And were you a sort of dark queen like in a story? And in the church where I went to say things to God there were pictures, old oil pic-tures that were in niches, of Our Lady with her child Jesus, and sometimes it was Our Lady of the Sorrows, and sometimes it was Our Lady of Budapest. And in the end I knew you were Our Lady of Sligo except you had lost your little boy and instead you had the sliver of your tattered girl, a coin of fear and sleeplessness in the palm of your bed.

OURSELVES ALONE
by Anne Devlin

Irish: Female

THE PLAY: Set in Northern Ireland, the complicated and intrigue-filled lives of a Republican family are given full view as the individuals plot, scheme, betray, and love amid the constant threat of being found out by British intelligence.

THE MONOLOGUE: Josie (25) is her father's daughter — a bit of a revolutionary and a fighter for the cause of a unified Ireland. When the cause gets a new British recruit, Joe, he must be interrogated to be sure that his motives are pure and trustworthy. Josie does the honors of the interrogation and explains her motivation to Joe.

TIME AND PLACE: Donna's flat in Anderstown, West Belfast. Northern Ireland. Present. Summer. Evening.

JOSIE: Let me tell you a story, Joe. When I was little my daddy used to say — "When the British withdraw we can be human." I believed that, since the south of Ireland was already free, there I could be human . . . Well, I'd been down south quite a few times, always to Bodenstown to the Wolfe Tone Commemorations and that meant coming back on the coach again as soon as it was over. One year when I was nearly sixteen, instead of coming straight back I stayed on and went to Dublin. I simply wanted to see the capital . . . I had no money and my shoes let in water, and I came back to Belfast at night with very wet feet in the back of a pig lorry. I smelt of pig feed. It dropped me off at seven-thirty in the morning on the Falls Road. I had time to go home and change before going to school at nine . . . There was a girl next to me in assembly. She had long straight fair hair and gleaming white teeth. If you leaned close she smelt of lemon soap. When she went to Dublin it was to buy clothes, she told me. I stood looking down at her beautifully polished shoes and I knew that it was all for her. Dublin existed for her to buy her shoes in . . . All day the smell of pig feed stayed with me . . . From then on I stopped wanting only British withdrawal — to unite Ireland for the shoppers and the shopkeepers of Belfast and Dublin. I became a revolutionary. You see it wasn't the presence of the

British that made me feel unclean that morning — it was the presence of money — Irish money as much as English money. Do you understand, Joe? What I want to know is, what are you doing in the ranks of the un-human? I was born here. *(Joe thinks for a minute, then reaches into his pocket, takes out his wallet, from which he quickly takes all the notes, and thrusts both wallet and notes into Josie's hands.)*

OURSELVES ALONE
by Anne Devlin

Irish: Female

THE PLAY: Set in Northern Ireland, the complicated and intrigue-filled lives of a Republican family are given full view as the individuals plot, scheme, betray, and love amid the constant threat of being found out by British intelligence.

THE MONOLOGUE: Donna's (25) husband Liam has finally been released from prison, and Donna finds her old anxiety attacks returning. She is visited again by the devil, who she hasn't seen since her husband went to prison. The complicated world of her family and friends has begun to affect her and her child, and she can't seem to shake it.

TIME AND PLACE: Donna's flat in Anderstown, West Belfast, Northern Ireland. Present. Summer. Evening.

Donna is sitting on a straight-backed chair, alone in the living room. There is a light on her face, the rest is darkness.

DONNA: The devil's back. He was lying with his head on my pillow this morning. When I woke up I recognized him immediately. Even though it's been years. *(Pause.)* The first time I ever saw him, he was standing in the corner of the room. I could feel something watching me. I had the bedclothes tucked up almost to my nose, so that I had to peer carefully round the room — and there he was. He seemed to grow out of the corner until he was towering over me. I panicked because I felt I was suffocating. My first husband was with me at the time. He called a doctor. He said I had asthma. The funny thing was, I really didn't get over my asthma attacks until my husband was interned. And I haven't seen the devil since. *(Pause.)* Until this morning. Liam bent over and kissed me good-bye as he was leaving. The trouble was he blocked my mouth and I couldn't breathe through my nose so I kept having to break away from him. When he'd gone, I closed my eyes and tried to get some sleep before the child woke. That was when I heard the door open. I thought Liam had come back so I opened my eyes, and there he was, the devil. If he had any hair at all it was red. He climbed on top of the bed and put his head on the pillow next to me. I felt so sick at the sight of him because I knew I didn't have the strength to struggle any more. I said: "Please leave me alone." I was very surprised when he replied. He's never spoken to me before. He said very quietly, "All right, Donna." And do you know — he vanished. But I don't believe he's really gone. He never really goes away.

THE STEWARD OF CHRISTENDOM
by Sebastian Barry

Irish: Female

THE PLAY: Traversing time both past and present, *The Steward of Christendom* tells the story of a retired Police captain and his three daughters in post–World War I Ireland. Now confined to a psychiatric home, Thomas Dunne's memories of his younger days keep him company in the bleak, dank room he inhabits.

THE MONOLOGUE: Dolly Dunne (17) is Thomas's youngest (and favorite) daughter. Of the three sisters, she is the most free. Encouraged along by her father, and without the discipline of a mother (hers died at birth), she is allowed to grow up without constraint. Here, she attempts to understand the cruelty she and her friends experienced in town when they saw the Irish troops off to the war. She receives no sympathy or understanding from her much more conservative sisters.

TIME AND PLACE: 1922. Dublin Castle. In the parlor. Early evening.

DOLLY: I was down at the North Wall with the Galligan sisters.

Mary Galligan was going out with one of the Tommies, and he and his troop were heading off home today, so we went down to see them off.

They were nice lads. There was a good crowd down there, and the Tommies were in high spirits, singing and so on. It was very joyful.

They're going from Ireland and they'll never be back, why shouldn't we say good-bye? Do you know every barracks in Ireland has lost its officers and men? Regiments that protected us in the war, who went out and left thousands behind in France. Willie's own regiment is to be disbanded, and that's almost entirely Dublin lads.

And I'll tell you. Coming home in the tram, up the docks road, Mary Galligan was crying, and we were talking kindly to her, and trying to comfort her, and I don't know what we said exactly, but this woman, a middle-aged woman, quite well-to-do, she rises up and stands beside us like a long streak of misery, staring at us. And she struck Mary Galligan on the cheek, so as she left the marks of her hand there. And she would have attacked me too, but that the conductor came down and spoke to the woman. And she said we were Jezebels and should have our heads shaved and be whipped, for following the Tommies. And the conductor looked at her, and hadn't he served in France himself, as one of the Volunteers, oh, it was painful, the way she looked back at him, as if he were a viper, or a traitor. The depth of foolishness in her. A man that had risked himself, like Willie, but that had reached home at last.

THE CRIPPLE OF INISHMAAN
by Martin McDonagh

Irish: Male

THE PLAY: Set on the remote Aran Island of Inishmaan, this rich, poignant story of a young man dreaming to escape the boundaries of his island life is at once compelling, humorous and ultimately stark and tragic.

THE MONOLOGUE: Cripple Billy (18) has just returned from his adventures in America, where he went to become an actor. He got to America, in part, by deceiving the villager Babbybobby. Upon his return, Babbybobby confronts the deceitful Billy, and Billy is left to explain himself. The stakes are high as Babbybobby is a very threatening man.

TIME AND PLACE: Inishmaan, Aran Islands. Ireland. 1934. Early evening. The local town hall after a showing of the film, *The Man of Aran.*

BILLY: I want to, Bobby. See, I never thought at all this day would come when I'd have to explain. I'd hoped I'd disappear forever to America. And I would've too, if they'd wanted me there. If they'd wanted me for the filming. But they didn't want me. A blond lad from Fort Lauderdale they hired instead of me. He wasn't crippled at all, but the Yank said "Ah, better to get a normal fella who can act crippled than a crippled fella who can't fecking act at all." Except he said it ruder. *(Pause.)* I gave it a go anyways. I had to give it a go. I had to get away from this place, Babbybobby, be any means, just like me mammy and daddy had to get away from this place. *(Pause.)* Going drowning meself I'd often think of when I was here, just to . . . just to end the laughing at me, and the sniping at me, and the life of nothing but shuffling to the doctor's and shuffling back from the doctor's and pawing over the same oul books and finding any other way to piss another day away. Another day of sniggering, or the patting me on the head like a broken-brained gosawer. The village orphan. The village cripple, and nothing more. Well, there are plenty round here just as crippled as me, only it isn't on the outside it shows. *(Pause.)* But the thing is, you're not one of them, Babbybobby, nor never were. You've a kind heart on you. I suppose that's why it was so easy to cod you with the TB letter, but that's why I was so sorry for codding you at the time and why I'm just as sorry now. Especially for codding you with the same thing your Mrs. passed from. Just I thought that would be more effective. But, in the long run, I thought, or I hoped, that if you had a choice between you being codded a while and me doing away with meself, once your anger had died down anyways, you'd choose you being codded every time. Was I wrong, Babbybobby? Was I?

A HANDFUL OF STARS
by Billy Roche

Irish: Male

THE PLAY: Life in a small town for a young man with ambitions and dreams can be a study in frustration and resignation. Jimmy is on the cusp of his future in a small town in Ireland, and all his hometown heroes are still home in the small town pool hall, drinking, playing, and dreaming their lives away. The memory of a good moment in his life gives him hope that he may find the same sense of joy and completion — perhaps with his love, Linda. But soon, the desperation of his existence becomes too much for him to bear, and he explodes in a rampage that sets his future in stone.

THE MONOLOGUE: Jimmy (17) is being pursued by the town police for beating up a bouncer at another pub, and for random acts of violence and vandalism throughout the town. He steals away to his favorite place, the pool hall, to catch his breath. His old friend Tony finds him and tries to get him to confess and turn himself in, but Jimmy's anger is unsettled. Tony watches in astonished horror as Jimmy breaks into the sacred back room where the good pool table lives and the older, high status clientele play pool — the place that Tony and Jimmy had always hoped to be invited.

TIME AND PLACE: The present. A small town in Ireland. A scruffy pool hall. Late evening.

JIMMY: Nobody's goin' to wrap me up in a nice neat little parcel. I'm not goin' to make it handy for you to forget about me — not you, not me Ma nor me Da, not Swan, nobody.
(Jimmy picks up a cue and holds it above his head. Tony cowers away from it. Jimmy turns and storms at the door to the back room and begins kicking it and hunching it with his shoulder. Eventually, as Tony gazes on in awe and disgust, Jimmy manages to break in, falling into the back room. We hear him wrecking the place in there, pulling down cupboards, kicking over chairs, scattering balls and breaking an out-of-sight window. When Jimmy appears in the doorway he has a frenzied look about him.)
Tell them Jimmy Brady done it. The same Jimmy Brady that's scrawled all over this town. Jimmy Brady who bursted that big bully of a bouncer with

a headbutt when everyone else was afraid of their livin' lives of him. The same Jimmy Brady that led Detective Garda Swan twice around the houses and back again . . . Yeh see that's the difference between me and Conway. He tiptoes around. I'm screamin'. Me and Stapler are screamin'. So if you want to join the livin' dead then go ahead and do it by all means Tony but don't expect me to wink at your gravediggers. Conway . . . the big he-man with no bell on his bike. I hates him I'm not coddin' yeh I do.

All right. It's not Conway's fault, it's not your fault, it's not Paddy's . . . Whose fault is it then Tony? Mine? Tell me who's to blame will yeh til I tear his friggin' head off.

Yeah right, it's nobody's fault. *(Jimmy plonks himself down hopelessly on the bench.)* It's nobody's fault. Everyone's to blame.

(There is a long painful silence. Jimmy lights up a cigarette and drags on it. Tony shuffles nervously across to the back room, eyeing the devastation, heart-broken. Jimmy looks up at him.)

Go ahead in Tony. Go on, be a man.

(Tony turns his back on the room, bowing his head in sadness.)

What's wrong with yeh Tony? I thought you were dyin' to get in there. I thought you'd be mad to play on the big snooker table or to try out one of the poker chairs. What's the matter with yeh? Are you afraid that the lads are like the three bears or somethin', that they'll come back and catch yeh?

THE LOVERS
by Brian Friel

Irish: Male

THE PLAY: Surprising and tragic, Brian Friel's look at the lives of two young lovers seems innocent enough, and then takes a surprising twist. Told in two parts, in the first section of the play, the action is taken by the young lovers as we hear the narration of the older lovers. The narration takes an "evening news broadcast" tone that starkly contrasts with the vibrancy and life of the lovers we watch. The tone proves to be effective in the set-up of the eventual tragedy. The second half of the play reverses the roles as the young lovers become the narrators of the older lovers' story.

THE MONOLOGUE: On a beautiful early summer afternoon, Joe and Mag (both 17) meet to study for their (GED) tests. Maggie, expecting Joe's baby soon, cannot seem to keep her thoughts on her books, but Joe, the soon-to-be-provider, is focused and disciplined in his study. Here, he takes a momentary breather before moving on to the next subject.

TIME AND PLACE: A hilltop in Ballymore (a fictional town). County Donegal. Ireland. Early afternoon. June 1966.

Joe has finished his calculation. He closes his books with a satisfied flourish.

JOE: Math's done! They can do their damndest now — I'm ready for them! I'll tell you something, Mag: you know when you're sitting in the exam hall and the papers have just been given out and your eye runs down the questions? Well, those are the happiest moments of my life. There's always that tiny uncertainty that maybe this time they'll come up with something that's going to throw you; but that only adds to the thrill because you know in your heart you're . . . invincible. *(He begins to put his books away: because he is on top of his work, he is in an expansive mood.)* I didn't tell you; I met old Skinny Skeehan: "I'll start you in my office, lad, as soon as your exams are over. On your mother's account I hope you're a good time-keeper and that your writing is legible." I never looked at him right before: his eyelids are purple and his ears are all hairy. So I just said to him:

"Stick your clerkship up your legal ass and get a lawnmower at those ears of yours" — like hell. But that's what I should have said, the hungry get. *(Mentally ticking off.)* About another hour to French and the same at history and I'll leave the English to tomorrow. Remember I was telling you how George Simpson got an extern degree at London University? Well, I wrote to them last night for a syllabus. Three years; that's all it takes. Joseph Brennan, Bachelor of Science. Then, by God, the world's our oyster. You asleep, Mag?

(Mag neither moves nor opens her eyes.)

THE LOVERS
by Brian Friel

Irish: Male

THE PLAY: Surprising and tragic, Brian Friel's look at the lives of two young lovers seems innocent enough, and then takes a surprising twist. Told in two parts, in the first section of the play, the action is taken by the young lovers as we hear the narration of the older lovers. The narration takes an "evening news broadcast" tone which starkly contrasts the vibrancy and life of the lovers we watch. The tone proves to be effective in the set-up of the eventual tragedy. The second half of the play reverses the roles as the young lovers become the narrators of the older lovers' story.

THE MONOLOGUE: On a beautiful early summer afternoon, Joe and Mag (both 17) meet to study for their (GED) tests. Maggie, expecting Joe's baby soon, cannot seem to keep her thoughts on her books, but Joe, the soon-to-be-provider, is focused and disciplined in his study. As Maggie naps, Joe makes plans for their future.

TIME AND PLACE: A hilltop in Ballymore (a fictional town). County Donegal, Ireland. Early afternoon. June 1966.

JOE: Mag, there is something I never told you. And since you are going to be my wife, I don't want there to be any secrets between us. I have a post-office book. I have had it since I was ten. And there is twenty-three pound fifteen in it now. I intend spending that money on a new suit, new shoes, and an electric razor. And I'm mentioning this to you now in case you suspect I have other hidden resources. I haven't. *(He cannot maintain this tone. He continues naturally.)* And I was working out our finances. The rent of the flat's two-ten. That'll leave us with about four-ten. And if I could get some private pupils, that would bring in another — say — thirty bob. We can manage fine on that, can't we? I mean, I can. What about you? *(Looks down at her.)* Mag? You asleep, Mag? How the hell can you sleep when you have no work done? Maggie? . . . *(He kneels beside her and looks into her face. He gently puts her hair away from her eyes. He straightens up as he remembers the word Caesarean.)* Dictionary . . . *(He gets his own dictionary and searches for the word.)* Cadet . . . cadge . . . Caesar . . .

Caesarean, pertaining to Caesar or the Caesars — section — an operation by which the walls of the stomach are cut open and . . . *(Shocked and frightened.)* . . . Cripes! *(Reads.)* As with Julius — oh, my God! If I see you on that bike again I'll break your bloody neck! As with Julius — good God! Maggie, are you all right, Maggie? O God, that's wild, wild! Sleep, Mag; that's bound to be good for you. *(He lifts her blazer and spreads it over her.)* There. God almighty! Cut open. *(Takes the blazer off.)* Maybe you'll be too warm. God, I'd sit ten exams every day sooner than this! Don't say a word, Maggie; just sleep and rest! That twenty-three pound fifteen — it's for you, Maggie. And I want you to — to — to squander it just as you wish: fur coats, dresses, perfumes, make-up, all that stuff — anything in the world you want — don't even tell me what you spend it on; I don't want to know. It's yours. And curtains for the window — whatever you like. God, Mag, I never thought for a minute it was that sort of thing! *(He looks closely at her.)* Mag . . . *(Whispers.)* Mag, I'm not half good enough for you. I'm jealous and mean and spiteful and cruel. But I'll try to be tender to you and good to you; and that won't be hard because even when I'm not with you — just when I think of you — I go all sort of silly and I say to myself over and over again: *I'm crazy about Maggie Enright;* and so I am — crazy about you. You're a thousand times too good for me. But I'll try to be good to you; honest to God, I'll try. *(He kisses her hand and replaces it carefully across her body. Then with sudden venom.)* Those Caesars were all gets! *(He takes an apple from one of the lunch bags, gets out his penknife, and peels it. As he does, he talks to Mag even though he knows she is asleep.)* I hope it's a girl, like you; with blond hair like yours. 'Cos if it's a boy it'll be a bloody hash, like me. And every night when I come home from Skeehan's office I'll teach her maths and she'll grow up to be a prodigy. I saw a program on TV once about an American professor who spoke to his year-old daughter in her cot in four different languages for an hour every day; and when the child began to talk she could converse in German, French, Spanish and Italian. Imagine if my aul fella looked down into our wee girl's cot and she shouted up to him: "Buenos dias!" Cripes, he'd think she was giving him a tip for a horse! I hope to God it's a girl. But if it's twins I'd rather have two boys or two girls than . . . *(He glances shyly at Maggie and tails off sheepishly when he realizes he has fallen into her speech pattern.)* . . . D'you hear me? That's the way married people go. They even begin to look alike. Wonder is old Skinny Skeehan married? I bet she looks like a gatepost . . . Your father, Mag, my God he's such a fine man. And your mother — I mean she's such a fine woman. I remember — oh, I was only a boy at the time — I remember seeing them walking together out the Dublin Road; and I thought they were so — you know — so dignified-looking. I'd like to be like him. God, such a fine man. And so friendly to everyone. You're lucky to have parents like that . . .

My aul fella — lifting the dole on a Friday — that's what he lives for. She laughs and calls him her man Friday; but I don't know how she can laugh at it. And to listen to him talking — cripes, you'd think he was bloody Solomon. How he can sit on his backside and watch her go out every morning with her apron wrapped in a newspaper under her arm — honest to God, I don't know how he does it. I said it to her once, you know; called him a loafer or something. And you should have seen her face! I thought she was going to hit me! "Don't you ever — ever — say the likes of that again. You'll never be half the man he is." Loyalty, I suppose; 'cos when you're that age, you hardly — you know — really love your husband or wife any more . . . Did I ever tell you what he does when there's no racing? He has this tin trunk under his bed; he keeps all my old school reports in it. And he sits up there in the cold and takes out the trunk and pores over all those old papers — term reports and all, away back to my primary-school days! Real nut! I know damn well when he's at it 'cos I can hear the noise of the trunk on the lino. And once when I went into the room he tried to stuff all the papers out of sight. Strange, too, isn't it . . . You know, we never speak at all, except maybe "Is the tea ready?" or "Bring in some coal" . . . Sitting up there in that freezing attic, going over my old marks . . .

Maybe when I'm older, maybe we'll go to football matches together, like Peadar Donnelly and his aul fella . . . I don't like football matches, but he does; and we shouldn't have to speak to each other — except going and coming back . . . Three years is no length for a degree. And I think myself I'd be a good teacher.

PHILADELPHIA, HERE I COME
by Brian Friel

Irish: Male

THE PLAY: Using the device of a public and a private persona, Brian Friel exposes us to two sides of the same man on the eve of his leaving Ireland for America.

THE MONOLOGUE: Gareth O'Donnell (25) has lived in Ballybeg (a fictional Donegal town) his whole life. After his girlfriend marries someone else, and his aunt and uncle invite him to live with them in America, he rashly makes the decision to leave his widowed father and head off to America. On his last night at home, he sits down to tea with his father and wishes that the conversation would be different, just this once. His thoughts are spoken by his private self who talks and acts just as if he could be seen and heard.

TIME AND PLACE: Mid-afternoon. The O'Donnell kitchen. Ballybeg, County Donegal, Ireland. The present.

PRIVATE: Ah! That's what we were waiting for; complete informality; total relaxation between intimates. Now we can carry on. Screwballs. *(Pause.)* I'm addressing you, Screwballs.
(He becomes more and more intense, and it is with an effort that he keeps his voice under control.)
Screwballs, we've eaten together like this for the past twenty-odd years, and never once in all that time have you made as much as one unpredictable remark. Now, even though you refuse to acknowledge the fact, Screwballs, I'm leaving you forever. I'm going to Philadelphia, to work in an hotel. And you know why I'm going, Screwballs, don't you. Because I'm twenty-five, and you treat me as if I were five — I can't order even a dozen loaves without getting your permission. Because you pay me less than you pay Madge. But worse, far worse than that, Screwballs, because — *we embarrass one another.* If one of us were to say, "You're looking tired" or "That's a bad cough you have," the other would fall over backways with embarrassment. So tonight d'you know what I want you to do? I want you to make one unpredictable remark, and even though I'll still be on that plane tomorrow

morning, I'll have doubts: Maybe I should have stuck it out; maybe the old codger did have feelings; maybe I have maligned the old bastard. So now, Screwballs, say . . . *(Thinks.)* . . . "Once upon a time a rainbow ended in our garden" . . . say, "I like to walk across the White Strand when there's a misty rain falling" . . . say , "Gar, son —" say, "Gar, you bugger you, why don't you stick it out here with me for it's not such a bad aul bugger of a place." Go on. Say it! Say it! Say it!

RED ROSES AND PETROL
by Joseph O'Connor

Irish: Male

THE PLAY: A family gathers once again for the funeral of their father. It has been many years, and many crises since the Doyle family has been together, and the reunion rekindles old sparks of anger.

THE MONOLOGUE: Johnny Doyle (20s) was his father's favorite, and therefore, his mother's favorite. He arrives at the house after the funeral mass to pay his respects. As the family waits for the other mourners to come over, Johnny tries to get the party going by telling jokes, torturing his sister's new boyfriend, and telling family secrets. Here, he reveals one of his keenest memories of his father.

TIME AND PLACE: Late afternoon, Doyle family living room. Dublin, Ireland. The present.

JOHNNY: Oh really, Ma. Don't you? Well, let's tell a few stories, will we? Seeing as nobody knows any jokes. I'll start. I used to rob shops, Tom, when I was a kid. My very expensive psychiatrist has explained to me that this was all my parents' fault, because they didn't give me enough attention. But I didn't know that at the time. I thought I used to rob shops because I was a robbing pure little bastard. But there I am anyway, in Eason's, one day, and up the jumper goes this big book of poetry. Yeats' poems. Father's Day is coming up, you see, and I've no readies for a present for The Da, so. Up the ganzee goes Willie B. And I'm on my way out the door, tap on the shoulder. Up to the manager's office quick march. Why did you do it, says he. I'm disturbed, says I. The manager rings up The Da. The Da comes in firing on all cylinders, guns blazing, I mean, open for fuckin' business, Tom. He bet me from one end of Abbey Street to the other. And do you know what he did then?
[TOM: What?]
JOHNNY: He took me down to the cop shop himself.
[MOYA: Stop, Johnny.]
JOHNNY: Down to Store Street. And I'm crying. I mean, I'm seven. And I'm so scared that I'm pissing in my pants, Tom. And I'm begging. Please,

Daddy, please, I'll never do it again. And what does The Da do? Up to the counter, knocks on it, knock, knock, knock. Big woollyback culchie guard sweating Irish stew into his armpits. What can I do for your honour? Would you ever lock this pup in a cell for the night, says The Da to the copper. I couldn't do that, sir, tis against the regulations. Out to the car, another few punches to the kidney, then home for round two. Good story isn't it? Will I go on? Do you want to hear what happened when I failed the leaving cert? Or maybe Catherine's told you.

RED ROSES AND PETROL
by Joseph O'Connor

Irish: Male

THE PLAY: A family gathers once again for the funeral of their father. It has been many years and many crises since the Doyle family has been together, and the reunion strikes sparks of old anger.

THE MONOLOGUE: Johnny Doyle (20s) was his father's favorite, and therefore, his mother's favorite. As the day has worn on, and no mourners have come to the house for the wake, the family gets more and more cruel and truthful to each other. After everyone else has stormed out of the living room, Johnny searches for some cocaine to ease his headache. He finds the envelope filled with his father's ashes in his sister's purse and, mistaking it for cocaine, snorts a line. He settles down to watch his dad on one of the videotapes he left when he died.

TIME AND PLACE: Late evening, Doyle family living room. Dublin, Ireland. The present.

JOHNNY: *(Laughing. He stares at his father's face on the screen.)* Well, Da, you know now. You know if there's anything up there now. You always wondered, didn't you? You said you knew for sure, but you always wondered. I knew that. You wanted everything to be sure. And you wanted everyone to be sure about you. But they weren't. Because you had your little secrets, didn't you, Da? Oh, you had your secrets all right.

(He brings a can of beer with him, sits down on the floor, and presses the play button.)

(Johnny pushes pause button.)

Remember that time I asked you if God was really there, do you? You poor old bastard. That time down in Connemara. It was late at night and we were walking up the boreen. It was pitch black and I had my hand in your hand. And we had torches, the two of us. You were smoking your pipe and when I shone my torch on your face you were smiling. And I asked you why. And you told me you were just happy. Happy. And I asked you why. And you said you were just happy to be here with your son. And we walked on a bit, and then I said to you, Daddy, is God just like Santa Claus? . . . And then you weren't happy any more, were you, Da? You weren't happy then. I'm so ashamed of you now, Johnny, you said. You've spoiled everything now. I'm so ashamed of you now for saying that.

(He sits back, watches the screen, presses the remote, and plays the videotape again.)

Enda Michael Malachi Doyle. You poor old fucking phoney.

(He pauses the screen again. He begins to sing softly.)

As I was climbing the scaffold high
My own dear father was standing by
But my own dear father did me deny.
And the name he gave me
Was The Croppy Boy.

THIS LIME TREE BOWER
by Conor McPherson

Irish: Male

THE PLAY: Told through a series of monologues, *The Lime Tree Bower* tells the story of two Irish brothers and their brother-in-law and the eventful "uneventful" lives they lead in their suburban Irish town. Frank (the elder brother) takes on the responsibility of caring for his father and his father's debts in a bold and illegal way. Joe (the younger brother) is coming to terms with his sexual awareness and the dynamics of relationships. Ray (the brother-in-law) is successful, handsome, married, and attempting to escape all the trappings his choice of life has brought him.

THE MONOLOGUE: After watching his best friend rape a girl in the cemetery, Joe (17) needs some cheering up. His brother Frank takes them both on a weekend holiday with the money he stole from the local loan shark. The brothers return home to find the police outside their father's café.

TIME AND PLACE: Present. A suburban city near Cork in Ireland. The café.

JOE: When we saw the guards, I think we all had the same idea.
  To put the foot down and get out of there.
  But it was too late. They saw us.
  It was horrible.
  Ray pulled over and a sergeant asked us to come in.
  There was a detective sitting with Dad in the front room. Dad looked wrecked.
  Carmel glared at us.
  Frank was white and his hands were shaking.
  But we were all completely wrong.
  Because it was me the detective wanted to talk to. He asked me if I knew a girl called Sarah Comisky.
  I didn't, I'd never heard the name.
  Then he asked me if I ever went to Shadows nightclub.
  I looked at Dad, but I had to say yes.
  He asked was I there the previous Sunday.
  I said I was and he nodded.

He just wanted to talk to me and Dad.

Everyone else had to go.

And when they were gone, he said I'd been accused of raping Sarah Comisky.

I nearly fell on the floor.

I said it wasn't me.

I didn't know any Sarahs.

But the detective told me to relax.

The girl hadn't accused me.

Damien had.

She had been attacked up in the graveyard near the Grange.

She had identified Damien as her attacker, but he said it was me.

The girl was very drunk but she did remember someone else being there.

So the guards wanted to find out if both of us had done it, or if one, which one.

Dad came with me down to the station and I had to give my account of what had happened. They made sure I got all the details right and then they gave me a cup of tea and a Kitkat.

Then Dad signed something, Then I did and they took a blood test.

Then we could go home.

I couldn't believe Damien had dropped me in it like that.

But Dad said I was too naive and that people would do anything to save their skin.

He said he knew it was disappointing but that was the way it was.

At home we all sat up late and talked about it and everyone was great.

We all drank beer until very late in the morning.

In bed that night I thought about my mother. It wasn't about the times when she couldn't talk and gave me nightmares.

It was about another time I'd forgotten.

Dad was teaching me how to skim stones on the beach. And Mum was trying to do it and she couldn't.

It was summer and she had a red dress on.

Dad was slagging her and she was laughing at herself.

And I felt safe and the safe feeling stayed.

I didn't go to school that week and the guards called on Tuesday to say that my test was negative.

They were charging Damien.

There was a bit of a shindig in the house.

Frank told me he was putting money away for me to go to college, but

I wasn't to say anything to Dad.

And Frank went to Chicago a few weeks later and he sent money back for Dad to pay off his loan.

Maybe he had a job, maybe he didn't.

Dad wasn't to know.

Ray brought a book out which nobody read.

But he was pleased.

He said that that was the point.

So in the end it was like things started off good, and just got better.

Is that cheating?

I don't know.

It's hard to say.

I can still see the girl.

SECTION THREE
RUSSIAN

RUSSIAN INTRODUCTION

The Russian people are long-suffering and incredibly warm and resilient. Russian history is filled with sorrow. The loss of Russian lives in war and revolutions is unequaled in many Western countries. The many changes of power, the ravage of the beautiful Russian environment by industry and population, and the legendary Russian winters all contribute to the stereotypical image of Russia as a bleak and harsh place filled with bleak and harsh people. Nothing could be further from the truth. If anything, the Russian tribulations have only served to strengthen and fortify the Russian sense of faith. Russians have an amazing ability, even when in the throes of ruin, to continue to hope that things will change for the better, soon.

The Russian culture is colorful and varied. Russian culture has set a standard of excellence in all areas of art. Many nations have attempted to achieve the esteem that the Russian art world holds, and few have ever surpassed its reputation. The Russian Ballet and dancers continue to hold the top spots on lists of "The All-Time Best." Russian music is deep, rich, and filled with the kind of soul that one would expect from a nation so deeply entrenched in sorrow and hardship. Russian authors, poets, playwrights, and teachers are known throughout the world for their pioneering styles and themes. Almost any American actor who has ever studied his or her craft can trace a few of his or her techniques back to the famous Russian acting teacher, Konstantin Stanislavski.

Post–cold war Russia is struggling toward a capitalistic, Westernized society. Images and essences of Western traditions are slowly creeping into the general Russian culture. The young people like to wear the same trendy clothes that young people worldwide wear. American and British television and films are an ever-present example of the world outside Russia. The young want to know and use Westernized words and phrases.

Just as in the other dialects studied, there exist many different kinds of Russian dialects that vary in strength and sound due to the geography, education, and experience of the speaker. There are many provinces in the former Soviet Republic, and to be spot on with your character's sound, you may need to do focused and specific research. For our purposes, we will study and play with some basic, overall sound changes prevalent in the Russian language.

As this is our first consideration of a dialect in which the native language of the speaker is not English, the strength of the accent will be determined by each individual speaker/character. In other words, you can be as fluent in English as you want to be. You can also have fun not being fluent in English. At any rate, your speech patterns will be altered greatly due to the Russian sounds and rhythm of a nonnative English speaker.

- The voice of the Russian comes from deep in the center of the body and "swims around" in the chest and throat region — creating a wonderfully deep rich resonant sound.
- The Russians are very deliberate in the way they speak. They commit to the energy they have at the top of their thought and continue to press on, even when grammatical errors come up.
- The Russian vowel sounds tend to be more guttural and long, perhaps giving them time during the speaking of the vowel to think about the next word in the sentence.
- Remember, this is an accent of a speaker whose native language is not English. This will cause some syntax errors or errors in the stressed syllables of the words.
- The sounds are not vastly different from the sounds we make in American English, but when coupled with the idea that English is not the native language, the delivery of the sounds will reveal the accent.
- Just think of speaking the words as they are spelled, without knowing the American rules for pronunciation (for example *ed* endings in American English come out sounding like *t,* but the Russians would sound out the *ed*).
- When all else fails, swallow your sounds and let the sounds vibrate in your chest.
- There is little mouth movement with the Russian accent; they tend to speak with the mouth mostly closed (another possible reason for the throat and chest resonance).

Russian Film, Television, and Audio References

Film

Rounders	John Malkovich
Air Force One	Gary Oldman (an actor doing a good accent)
The Cutting Edge	The coach
White Knights	Mikhail Baryshnikov, Helen Mirren
Turning Point	Mikhail Baryshnikov
Company Business	Mikhail Baryshnikov
Moscow on the Hudson	Robin Williams (he's pretty good with all dialects)
Anastasia	Disney version, listen to the smaller characters
The Russian House	Klaus Brandauer, Michelle Pfeiffer (she does pretty well)
To Russia with Love	Russian bad guys
Reds	Genuine Russian interviews
Back in the U.S.S.R.	Real Russians
Citizen X	

Television

"Bullwinkle"	Boris and Natasha

Dialect Tapes and Books

Stage Dialects and More Stage Dialects	Jerry Blunt
Dialects for the Stage	Evangeline Machlin
Acting with an Accent/Russian	David Alan Sterns
IDEA website	www.ukans.edu/~idea/index.html

For a more complete and detailed list of films/resources, see Ginny Kopf's book The Dialect Handbook.

Russian Sounds

- Russian accent vowel changes:

ih → ee	his → heez
ee → ih	speech → spihch
er → air (very throaty)	words → vairds
a → ah (or) eh	back → bahk/behk
aw → ow	thought → thowt
(ed endings are sounded out)	looked → lookid

- Russian consonant changes:

[r] trilled before vowels	rate, right, red
[th] → [d]	this, these → dis, dhese
[th] → [t]	thanks, think → tanks, tink
[w] → [v]	with, was, watch → vith, vas, vatch
[v] → [f]	very, movie → fery, moofie
ing + k	singing → singingk
[h] made in throat with a lot of air	house, head
[d] at the end of a word gets an extra [t]	mind → mindt
intrusive [w]	gold, fold → gwold, fwold
intrusive [y]	get, kept, lend → gyet, kyept, lyend

RUSSIAN PRACTICE SENTENCES

[ih] → [ee]:
    His trip to Israel was important to him. This is his distant cousin,
    Leonid.

[ee] → [ih]:
    Her speech is neat, what a treat. These are for Cleveland and Sweden.
    I want meat.

[er] → [air]:
    We heard the word that she learned the bird's song. Birds are early risers.

[a] → [ah/eh]:
    That was the plan for the man at the stand. She had her hand in the
    bad man's bag.

[aw] → [ow]:
    They thought the cop caught the lout but they thought wrong.

[r]:
    Red roses and rhubarb are really remarkable. Ride the river on the raft.

[th] → [d]:
    This is the brother of the mother's brother. Is that what they wanted?

[th] → [t]:
    Thanks for thinking of things. Throw the ball through the third
    window.

[d] → [dt]:
    Leonid and Ovid were bad men. Worldwide bread is bad for the head.

[v] → [f]:
    The glove of the lover was in the cave. Save the wave for the rave.

[ing + k]:
>
> Walking and talking was killing the meeting. With singing, we are playing.

[h]:
>
> Have some homemade hummus. Help the host have the happy hero's holiday.

[w] → [v]:
>
> We are winning the war of the windows. Where is the weather worker?

intrusive [w]:
>
> They told the golden old man the old lonely rope story.

intrusive [y]:
>
> He kept the solemn book. She will get him to lend it.

THE LOVE-GIRL AND THE INNOCENT
by Alexander Solzhenitsyn

Russian: Female

THE PLAY: Set in a co-ed prison in the autumn of 1945, *The Love-Girl and the Innocent* reveals the inner workings and politics behind the paranoid cold war Russian policies. Most of the prisoners had come from the Russian front where they were fighting to save their country in World War II. They then found themselves labeled "enemies of the state" for disagreeing, or not actively agreeing, with the new Soviet system of government.

THE MONOLOGUE: Lyuba (23), the love-girl, has grown attached to Nemov and they steal a moment backstage at the prison play to learn more about each other.

TIME AND PLACE: Autumn, 1945. A prison work camp. Backstage during a prison group performance.

LYUBA: I was six. I remember a huge barge full of dispossessed *kulak* farmers. There were no partitions in the hold, no tiered bunks. People just lay on top of other people. Maybe it was because I was small, but the walls of the barge seemed to tower over me like cliffs. Guards with guns walked around the top edge. Our whole family was exiled, but our two elder brothers weren't living with us, so they weren't touched. They came to the transit camp. The boat had just left and they tried to catch up with us. All the time they were on the lookout for a chance to get their family out of trouble. They didn't succeed. But they managed to buy me from the escort commander. They gave him a shirt with a zip — they were just coming into fashion. I don't remember how they got me off the barge, but I remember we were in a little boat, and the water shone brightly in the sun.

You can't imagine how we lived after that. I had no room, so I lived five years in a bit of dark corridor. There was no window and I couldn't do my homework after school. I went to school every day hungry and dressed like a beggar. I couldn't complain or ask for help in case people found out we were *kulaks*. But I wanted pretty dresses, I wanted to go to the cinema . . . My brother married. He has his own children . . . They married me off when I was fourteen . . .

MARRIAGE
by Nikolai Gogol

Russian: Female

THE PLAY: Described by the author as "a completely unlikely incident in two acts," *Marriage* is a comic look at the old tradition of matchmaking. Fyokla is the town's local matchmaker, and she is preparing to get a husband for the beautiful, young Agafya. On her list of potential mates is the confirmed and stubborn bachelor, Podkolyosin. With the added intrusion of Podkolyosin's friend Kochkaryov, and the roomful of eager suitors, Fyokla has her hands full. The happy ending is quite possibly what the author meant by "unlikely."

THE MONOLOGUE: Agafya (20s) has spent only a few minutes in her sitting room with a bevy of suitors all trying to win her affection. She was too startled and overwhelmed to say much, and darted from the room. Now, alone in her room, she wonders at her choices and can't seem to make up her mind.

TIME AND PLACE: Agafya's room, in her house behind the dressmaker's house, in back of the beer hall. A small town in Russia near a bigger town in Russia. Anytime.

Agafya Tikhonovna is alone.

AGAFYA: It's impossible to choose! If it were only one gentleman, or two. But four! I simply don't know which one. Nikanor Ivanovitch Anuchkin isn't bad looking . . . he's thin, of course. Ivan Kuzmitch Podkoliosin's not so bad either. On the other hand, Ivan Pavlovitch Poach'Tegg may be fat, but he is impressive. Baltazar Baltazarovitch Zhevakin's a strong contender . . . oh, it's too hard to make such a crucial decision. If you put Anuchkin's lips under Podkoliosin's nose . . . or combined Zhevakin's manners with Poach'Tegg's solidity — then there'd be no question of choice. But as things stand, the whole business is giving me a headache! Perhaps it would be best to draw lots and leave it in God's hands. I'll write their names on scraps of paper, fold them up and . . . and Thy will be done! *(She tears up a sheet of paper, writes names on the scraps, folds them as she talks.)* What a miserable position for a young girl, particularly if she's in love. Men are never placed in such a position — they can't begin to grasp the difficulty of her situation. Done. Well, let me put them in my purse . . . I close my eyes . . . and what will be will be. *(She places her hand in the purse.)* I pray I get Nikanor Ivanovitch Anuchkin. Wait, why do I want him? Ivan Kuzmitch Podkoliosin's a better choice, Podkoliosin? No, he's worse than all the rest. No . . . no . . . let fate decide. *(She draws all the scraps out at once.)* All of them? Impossible! My heart's beating like a drum. I can only have one. *(She puts the scraps back into the purse. Kochkariev sneaks up behind her.)* Ah, if I could pick Baltazar Baltazarovitch — I mean Nikanor Ivanovitch —

MARRIAGE
by Nikolai Gogol

Russian: Female

THE PLAY: Described by the author as "a completely unlikely incident in two acts," *Marriage* is a comic look at the old tradition of matchmaking. Fyokla is the town's local matchmaker, and she is preparing to get a husband for the beautiful, young Agafya. On her list of potential mates is the confirmed and stubborn bachelor, Podkolyosin. With the added intrusion of Podkolyosin's friend Kochkaryov, and the roomful of eager suitors, Fyokla has her hands full. The happy ending is quite possibly what the author meant by "unlikely."

THE MONOLOGUE: Ágafya (20s) has been wooed (quickly) and won by Podkolyosin. Now, alone, she envisions her future as a married woman.

TIME AND PLACE: Agafya's room, in her house "behind the dressmaker's house, in back of the beer hall." A small town in Russia near a bigger town in Russia. Anytime.

AGAFYA: My heart's still pounding. No matter which way I turn, Ivan Kuzmitch seems to be standing there. That's it, then, there's no escaping one's fate. I must get him off my mind. But no — I try to wind my wool or embroider my purse, and Ivan Kuzmitch always seems to seize my hands and stop me. Maidenhood, adieu. They'll call for me, lead me to the altar, then leave me all alone with . . . a man! Oh, I'm trembling. Farewell to innocence, to my beautiful girlhood. *(In tears.)* How many years have I spent in peace, and now I must end it all. I must marry. There'll be nothing but trouble: noisy, quarrelsome little boys. And little girls who must be cared for, so that they can grow up and get married (may their husbands be kind men!). But they might marry drunkards . . . no, I can't bear it! I haven't had enough time to enjoy my girlhood. I've only had twenty-seven years as a virgin . . . *(Voices off.)* Why is Ivan Kuzmitch so late? *(Podkoliosin is pushed through the door by Kochkariev.)*

THE SEAGULL
by Anton Chekhov

Russian: Female

THE PLAY: Chekhov's classic play about the lives and loves of a theatrical family and the havoc that the pursuit of art wreaks on their relationships with each other is not traditionally done in a Russian dialect, but the poetry and imagery of the text will be useful for the actor to explore.

THE MONOLOGUE: In this famous monologue, Nina (21) has returned to the country from Moscow. She is cold, hungry, poor, and a little unstable mentally. Here she meets up with her old friend and admirer, Treplov.

TIME AND PLACE: Sorin's country estate. Winter. Evening. Treplov's study.

NINA: Why do you say you kiss the ground I walk on? I ought to be killed. *(Leans against the table.)* I'm so exhausted. If only I could rest, just rest. *(Lifts her head.)* I'm a seagull! . . . No, that's not it. I'm an actress. Yes, that's right! *(She hears Arkadina and Trigorin's laughter, listens, then runs to the left door and looks through the keyhole.)* So, he is here, too . . . *(Turns to Treplev.)* Ah well . . . what does it matter . . . Yes . . . he never believed in the theater, you know, he always laughed at my dreams, and little by little I stopped believing and lost faith, too . . . And then there were the pressures of love, the jealousy, the constant worry over my little one . . . I became — I don't know — mediocre, pitiful, my acting made no sense any more . . . I didn't know what to do with my hands, how to stand on stage, how to control my own voice. You have no idea how it feels, to know you're acting badly. I'm a seagull. No that's not it . . . Do you remember, when you shot the seagull? "One day, by chance, there came a man who saw her and, for lack of anything better to do, destroyed her" . . . An idea for a short story . . . No, that's not it . . . *(Rubs her forehead.)* What was I saying? . . . Oh yes, I was talking about the stage. No, I'm not like that any more . . . I'm a true actress now, and I perform with joy, with ecstasy, I'm intoxicated on the stage, and I feel beautiful. And now, while I've been staying here, I've been walking, walking and thinking, thinking and feeling, how my spirit is growing stronger every day . . . And now I know, I understand, Kostya, that in our work — it's all the same, whether we perform or we write — the main thing is not the glory, not the glitter, no, not any of those things I dreamed of, it's having the strength to endure. The strength to bear your cross, to have faith. I have faith, and it's not so painful for me any more, and when I think about my calling, I'm not so afraid of life. I'm not.

THE SHADOW
by Evgeny Shvarts

Russian: Female

THE PLAY: Set in a fictional time and place, this play has been described as "a satire, an ode, and, perhaps, even partly a fable." (From the introduction to the play in *An Anthology of Russian Plays,* edited, translated, and introduced by F. D. Reeve. The quote is attributed to Lidiya Chukovskaya.) A Scholar, eager to experience the adventures of his idol, Hans Christian Andersen, ventures to the same place he did and encounters an odd group of people. It is a country where the fairy tales are reality, and logic makes no sense. The Scholar soon loses his Shadow and spends the rest of the play trying to get everything to end up happily ever after.

THE MONOLOGUE: Annunziata (17) is the hotel owner's daughter. She likes the Scholar and wants to warn him about her town's secret blessing and curse. Here she describes the magic of her hometown in an effort to caution the Scholar against believing in the happy endings the fairy tales usually promise.

TIME AND PLACE: A southern country. A hotel room. Anytime. Anyplace.

ANNUNZIATA: [I'm glad of that, thank you.] You're always nice to me. Probably I heard voices in the room next door and got it all confused. But . . . you won't get angry at me? Can I tell you something?

I've wanted to warn you about something for a long time . . . Don't be angry . . . You're a scholar, and I'm just a simple girl. But it's just . . . I can tell you something I know which you don't. *(Curtsies.)* Excuse me being so forward.

[I'm glad of that, thank you.] *(Looks around at the door.)* In the books about our country there's a lot written about the healthful climate, fresh air, wonderful views, hot sun, well . . . in short, you yourself know what's written in the books about our country . . .

Sure. You know what's written about us in the books, but what's not written about us there, you don't know.

You don't know that you're living in a wholly special country. Everything that's told as happening in fairy tales, everything that in other nations seems made up — actually occurs here every day. Why, for example, Sleeping Beauty used to live just a five hours' walk from the tobacco store — from the one that's on the right of the fountain. Only now Sleeping Beauty is dead. The Ogre is still alive and working as an appraiser in the municipal pawnshop. Tom Thumb married a very tall woman nicknamed Grenadier, and their children are people of normal height, just like you and me. And you know what's surprising? That woman nicknamed Grenadier is completely under his thumb. She even takes him to the market with her. Tom Thumb sits in the pocket of her apron and haggles away for all he's worth. However, they get on very well together. The wife is so considerate toward her husband. Whenever they dance a minuet on the holidays, she puts on extra glasses so as not to step on her man accidentally.

(Glancing at the door.) Not everybody likes fairy tales.

Indeed, can you imagine! *(Glances round at the door.)* We're terribly afraid that if everybody finds this out, they'll stop coming to us. That would be such a disadvantage! Don't give us away, please.

If it were children who came here, that would be one thing. But grown-ups are a cautious lot. They very well know that many fairy tales end sadly. That's just what I wanted to talk to you about. Be careful.

STARS IN THE MORNING SKY
by Alexander Galin

Russian: Female

THE PLAY: Set in cold war Russia during the 1980 Olympic games, this play reveals the desperation inherent in the lives of some of Moscow's "professional women." In an effort to put on a respectable front to the rest of the world, the Soviet government removed suspected criminals and ladies of the night from the streets of Moscow during the Olympic games. They were shuttled out to old hospitals-turned-retreat-centers and were basically held in a sort of house arrest.

THE MONOLOGUE: Laura (20s) has been relocated to a retreat center. Insistent that she is not like the other girls and that she has chosen to come up to the country for a rest, she separates herself from the rest of the residents. Only Alexander, the local crazy man, appeals to her. She can talk to him and feel safe with him. She reveals herself to him.

TIME AND PLACE: 1980. Summer. A former mental hospital in the countryside overlooking a river. Afternoon.

LAURA: Life's full of surprises, as some great writer said. Who was it? Stendhal, I think . . . Granny used to say when I was little I always ran around with my arms out . . . They said if you dreamt of flying it meant you were growing. I tried to fly when I was awake too, but I never did manage to grow. I jumped off mountains, flew over the sea . . . I still have those dreams sometimes.

　　It's all right for loonies, they can lie on clouds when they want to. My story's quite simple — I'm a trapeze artist. In the circus all my life. When I was little my parents used to saw me in half. I was nice and small, and I'd nip out of one box into another . . . But now I'm a trapeze artist. I'd like to do my act in Moscow. How d'you like the idea? I'm all in red, being thrown from hand to hand like a relay baton. Not bad, eh?

　　Listen, you're my last *chance!* I wondered why I liked talking to you so much. Because you're my *chance!* D'you know what's so unusual about you, Sasha? You know how to listen. Men never listen to women. Bed's all they can think of. That's all right in the end, but it's nice you've waited so long to make a pass at me. I thought you'd be rough, but not at all — if anything you're too gentle . . . Am I beginning to lose my touch, I wonder, doctor?

Stop, don't . . . I'm nothing really, just a nice piece of skirt . . .God, how I chatter on! I can't even talk decently any more! Nothing but the circus, tours and being tired . . . Now don't try anything yet. Just stay sweet and gentle, for a while, anyway . . . But no kissing, all right?

STARS IN THE MORNING SKY
by Alexander Galin

Russian: Female

THE PLAY: Set in cold war Russia during the 1980 Olympic games, this play reveals the desperation inherent in the lives of some of Moscow's "professional women." In an effort to put on a respectable front to the rest of the world, the Soviet government removed suspected criminals and ladies of the night from the streets of Moscow during the Olympic games. They were shuttled out to old hospitals-turned-retreat-centers and were basically held in a sort of house arrest.

THE MONOLOGUE: Maria (20s) has fallen in love with the hotel-owner's son, Nikolay. With her shady past (an illegitimate child being kept in another hostel) and her grim future, she is not Nikolay's mom's first choice for a daughter-in-law. As the Olympic torch finds its way across the countryside, near the girls' hostel, she agrees to go out with some traveling men as long as they promise to stop on the overpass so she can watch the torch go by. When the men drive past the overpass, Maria jumps out of the moving car. She is gravely injured and lies in bed hallucinating.

TIME AND PLACE: 1980. Summer. A former mental hospital in the countryside overlooking a river. Night.

MARIA: Anna, Larissa! I've been having such a funny dream! *(Laughs.)* There was this woman in our village who was terribly mean . . . she refused to have children, because they were such an expense . . . there are bitches like that. Her husband did odd jobs all round the village . . . She used to hire him out — not as a stud, as you're thinking, Anna! — he dug the pits when people wanted to build cellars, helped with the hay making . . . Anyway, she wore him to a shred. One of her schemes was to distill moonshine in the washing machine, using the spin dryer . . . But machinery needs energy, and the electricity is metered and costs money. So she went into the nearest town and traded sour cream for some crocodile clips to clip onto the power line direct and bypass the meter. *(Laughs.)* Honestly . . . I'm telling you — she did . . . Well one night some girls and I were coming back from a dance . . . and as we got near the village we saw something bright — at first we thought it was a shooting star. Then as we came closer, Katya shouted: "It's a spaceman!" And we ran toward him for all we were worth!

Poor chap, he'd climbed up on the pole to the cables . . . to the crocodile clips . . . and he must have touched the wrong thing, because he was shaking and giving off silver sparks like an angel . . . They didn't get him down till next morning . . . Ever since then he can't stop jerking and swaying from side to side, like a pendulum. But she even turned that to good use: whenever anyone in the village was pickling cabbage to make sauerkraut, she would take him there . . . tie a knife into his fist and sit him down. And he'd slice away at the cabbage like a machine.

THE STORM
by Alexander Ostrovsky

Russian: Female

THE PLAY: With the impending storm serving as a metaphor for the actions to come in the play, the characters in Ostrovsky's drama are full of the turbulence and unpredictability of the weather. Young lovers, old meddlers, and the decline of civilization are at the forefront of this tragedy. Boris is beholden to his wealthy uncle and must do his bidding to secure his inheritance. Katerina is married to a man she does not love and who feels no passion for her. As the townsfolk come in and out of the scenes exclaiming the lack of morality and the pervasive hypocrisy that is rampant amongst the rest of the citizens, Boris and Katerina consummate their love and it serves to ruin them both.

THE MONOLOGUE: Katerina (18 to 20) reveals her secret self to her sister-in-law and dearest friend, Varvara.

TIME AND PLACE: Summer. Kalinov, Russia (on the banks of the Volga). 1850s. In town.

KATERINA: *(Silence.)* Guess what I was just wondering.

Why people don't fly?

I mean, why don't people fly like birds? Sometimes I fancy I am a bird. When I stand on top of a hill I want so dreadfully to fly! I'd take a little run, spread out my arms and fly away. Shall I try it now? *(Starts forward, as if about to.)*

(With a sigh.) How full of life I used to be! I've quite wilted since I began living with you.

You should have seen me! I lived with nothing to trouble me, free as a bird. My mama loved me above everything else; she dressed me up like a doll and never pressed duties upon me, I did only what I wanted to do. Would you like to know how I lived in my maiden days? Listen, I will tell you. I used to get up early in the morning, and if it was summertime I would go down to the spring to wash and fill my bucket and come back and water all the plants in the house, and I had lots and lots of plants, Varvara. Then mother and I would go to church and all the pilgrims with us — our house was full of pilgrims and pious old ladies too. When we came back from service we would sit down to our work, mostly embroidering gold on velvet, and the pilgrims would recount where they had been and what they had seen and would tell us the lives of the saints or sing hymns. This would occupy us until dinner. After dinner the old ladies would lie down and I would go into the garden. Then we would attend vespers and in the evening again there would be tales and singing. You've no idea what a good life it was!

Ah, but here it is all as if forced on you. How I did love to go to church! Each time it was as if I entered paradise, and I was not aware of the people around me, or of the passage of time, or of the ending of the service. It might have been but a single moment. Mama used to say the whole congregation looked at me in wonder. Just think, Varya! On sunny days the light would stream down through the windows of the dome in a bright column, and smoke from the incense would form clouds in this column of light, and as if angels were flying and singing among these clouds. And then again, Varvara, I would get up at night, and in our house, too, lamps burned in front of the icons day and night, and I would kneel in a corner and pray until morning. Or I would go out into the garden early in the morning when the sun was just coming up and fall on my knees and weep and pray and not know myself what I was weeping and praying for. And there they would find me. I cannot think what I asked for in my prayers, for I was in need of nothing, I had all my heart could desire. And what dreams I had, Varvara, what dreams! Golden temples, and fairy-tale gardens, and invisible voices singing, and a fragrance as of cypress, and trees and hills like are painted on the holy images and not at all like in real life. And again as if I was flying, flying, way up in the air . . . I still have such dreams, but not very often and not the same.

THE STORM
by Alexander Ostrovsky

Russian: Female

THE PLAY: With the impending storm serving as a metaphor for the actions to come in the play, the characters in Ostrovsky's drama are full of the turbulence and unpredictability of the weather. Young lovers, old meddlers, and the decline of civilization are at the forefront of this tragedy. Boris is beholden to his wealthy uncle and must do his bidding to secure his inheritance. Katerina is married to a man she does not love and who feels no passion for her. As the townsfolk come in and out of the scenes exclaiming the lack of morality and the pervasive hypocrisy that is rampant amongst the rest of the citizens, Boris and Katerina consummate their love and it serves to ruin them both.

THE MONOLOGUE: Katerina (18 to 20) has been given the key (literally) to her happiness — Varvara has plotted to have Katerina's love-interest meet her in the secured and secret garden on her mother's property . . . all Katerina has to do is unlock the gate and wait for Boris.

TIME AND PLACE: Summer. Kalinov, Russia (on the banks of the Volga). 1850s. The sitting room of Katerina's mother-in-law's house (where Katerina also lives with her husband and sister-in-law).

KATERINA: *(Alone, with the key in her hand.)* What is she doing? What is she thinking of? Is she mad? Yes, mad, that's what she is! My ruin; here it is, in my own hand. I'll throw it away, throw it far away, into the river, so that nobody will ever find it. Ah, dear God, it burns my fingers like a live coal. *(After some consideration.)* That's how we women come to a bad end. Is it a pleasure, think you, being locked up like this? Naturally, all sorts of ideas come into your head. Then a chance of escape comes along; some women are only too glad to seize it, rush in without thinking. How is it possible, without thinking, without weighing the consequences? Ruin is but a step away! Weep, then, and suffer torment the rest of your life! Imprisonment will only seem the more bitter. *(Silence.)* It *is* bitter, never to be able to do anything you want, oh, how bitter! Who doesn't shed tears over it? And none weep so much as we women do.

Take me, now: I live in misery day after day, without seeing a ray of light and never hoping to. The longer I live the worse it gets. And now I have this sin on my conscience. *(Becomes lost in thought.)* If it wasn't for my mother-in-law . . . she's the one who has crushed me. It's because of her I've come to hate this house; the very walls are hateful. *(Gazes pensively at the key.)* Throw it away? Aye, I must throw it away. How did it ever fall into my hands? Here is temptation. Here is my ruin. *(Becomes suddenly alert.)* Someone is coming! How my heart is beating! *(Thrusts the key into her pocket.)* Nobody. A false alarm. How terrified I was! And I hid the key away. Well, then, that is what I was meant to do. That is my fate. After all, what harm can come from seeing him just once, if only from a distance? Or from speaking to him just once? But I promised my husband. Well, he didn't want to help me. Perhaps I will never have such a chance again. Blame yourself, then; the chance came and you were afraid to take it. What am I saying? Why am I trying to deceive myself? I would gladly die just to see him once! Why am I pretending? Throw the key away? Never, not for anything in the world! It belongs to me now. Come what may, I shall see Boris! Oh, if only night would come quickly!

THE STORM
by Alexander Ostrovsky

Russian: Female

THE PLAY: With the impending storm serving as a metaphor for the actions to come in the play, the characters in Ostrovsky's drama are full of the turbulence and unpredictability of the weather. Young lovers, old meddlers, and the decline of civilization are at the forefront of this tragedy. Boris is beholden to his wealthy uncle and must do his bidding to secure his inheritance. Katerina is married to a man she does not love and who feels no passion for her. As the townsfolk come in and out of the scenes exclaiming the lack of morality and the pervasive hypocrisy that is rampant amongst the rest of the citizens, Boris and Katerina consummate their love and it serves to ruin them both.

THE MONOLOGUE: Katerina (18 to 20) and Boris have been seeing each other for ten days while Katerina's husband (Tichon) has been away. Tichon returned unexpectedly and, in her guilt, Katerina confessed her infidelity. Now, as her love is banished from the town by her uncle and she is treated as a pariah by her family and townsfolk, Katerina bemoans her fate and foreshadows her doom.

TIME AND PLACE: Summer. Kalinov, Russia (on the banks of the Volga). 1850s. The sitting room of Katerina's mother-in-law's house (where Katerina also lives with her husband and sister-in-law).

The stage is empty a little, then from the other side Katerina comes on softly and wanders about.

KATERINA: *(Alone.)* Nowhere. Nowhere to be found. What could he be doing now, poor darling? Only to say good-bye to him, only that, and then . . . then I'm even ready to die. Why have I done this to him? It hasn't eased my lot any. Why couldn't I have met my fate alone? Alas, I've ruined myself and him too, brought dishonour on myself, eternal disgrace to him; yes, yes, dishonour on myself, eternal disgrace to him. *(Pause.)* Let me recall what he said to me, what tender words he spoke to me. What were they now? *(Takes her head in her hands.)* Ah, me, I can't remember. I've forgotten everything. It's the nights, the nights that are so terrible! Everyone goes to bed, and I go too; everyone sleeps, but I lie there like in my grave. How fearful the darkness is! I hear noises, and singing, like at a funeral; only so soft I can hardly catch the sound, and far, far away . . . When the morning light comes, what a relief! But I don't want to get up; the same people, the same talk, the same torture. Why do they look at me like that? Why don't they kill people nowadays? Why did they stop? They used to kill ones like me in the days gone by, they say. They would have taken me and thrown me into the Volga. And a good thing; I would have been glad. But nowadays they say "If we kill you, your sin will be atoned for; no, you must go on living and suffering for your sin!" Oh, I *am* suffering! How much longer will it go on? Why should I live? What have I to live for? There is nothing I want, nothing that pleases me, not even the light of day. But death doesn't come. I cry out for it, and it doesn't come. Everything I see and hear only makes the pain here *(Putting her hand on her heart.)* worse. Perhaps I would find some joy in life if I lived with him. And why shouldn't I? It makes no difference now, I am already a lost soul. How I long for him! Dear God, how I long for him! If I cannot see you, love, at least hear me from a distance! Sweet wind, carry to him my sorrow and my longing! Blessed saints, how I long for him! *(Goes to the riverbank and cries out in a loud voice.)* My love! My life! My soul! How I love you! Oh, answer me! Answer me! *(She weeps.)*

THE WHITE GUARD
(or The Days of the Turbins)
by Mikhail Afanasyevich Bulgakov

Russian: Male

THE PLAY: Set in the time of the Russian Revolution, as the Bolsheviks were clamoring to create a Soviet Union, and the Cossacks were marauding, the Ukrainian armed forces stood behind their Hetman (leader/prince). When even he deserted his capital, the people were left to see which side would win out and which government would lead them. The original alliances of the Turbin family are challenged and changed by the end of the play.

THE MONOLOGUE: Aleksei (30) is the oldest son in the family. As his sister's husband deserts the cause, and the people of Russia become more and more apathetic to the potential insurgence of the Germans, Aleksei maintains his strong feelings for his country and the cause of political reform. He attempts to inspire his comrades to follow his example.

TIME AND PLACE: Elena's drawing/sitting room. Evening. Winter, 1918. Kiev.

ALEXEI: Just a moment, gentlemen! What is happening? Are we being made fools of, or what? If instead of putting on this absurd comedy of Ukrainisation your Hetman had begun forming officers' volunteer detachments in time, then you wouldn't have seen hide nor hair of Petlyura in the Ukraine. And not just that: We would have swatted those Bolsheviks in Moscow like flies. And now would be the time to do it, by all accounts: I hear they're eating cats in Moscow. And he could have saved Russia!

[SHERVINSKY: The Germans wouldn't have allowed the Hetman to form an army, because they were afraid of it.]

ALEXEI: [I beg to differ.] We should have made it clear to the Germans that we were no threat to them. That's all over. We've lost the war. What faces us now is something more terrible than the war or the Germans, more terrible than anything else in the world: the Bolsheviks. We ought to have said to the Germans: "What do you need? Do you want wheat, sugar? Go on, take it, stuff yourself with it until you burst — only help us, help us to make sure our peasants don't catch the Moscow disease." But now it's too late; by now our officers have degenerated into barflies. An army of bar-room spongers! Just try getting one of them to fight now. Like hell he'll fight! His pockets are stuffed with black market foreign currency, he spends all day sitting in a cafe on the Kreshchatik, surrounded by a para-sitic horde of guards officers with cushy jobs at headquarters. Then one fine day they give Colonel Turbin an artillery regiment: panic, rush, hurry, form a unit from scratch, Petlyura's coming! . . . Oh, splendid! . . . I give you my word of honour that when I saw my recruits yesterday, for the first time in my life my heart sank into my boots.

My heart sank because for every hundred officer cadets I'd been given a hundred and twenty students, who didn't know one end of a rifle from the other. And yesterday on the parade ground . . . It was snowing, there was fog in the distance . . . I had a sudden feeling, you know, that I was going to a funeral . . .

[YELIENA: Alyosha, why do you say such dreadful, gloomy things? Stop it!]

[NIKOLKA: Don't worry, colonel, we'll never give in.]

ALEXEI: The fact is, as I sit here amongst you all, I'm obsessed by one thought: God, if only we could have foreseen all this earlier! Do you know what this Petlyura is? He's a myth, a black fog. He doesn't exist. Look out of the window and see what's there. A snowstorm, shadows, that's all . . . there are only two real forces in Russia, gentlemen: the Bolsheviks and us. And these two forces will clash before long. I see even blacker times ahead. I see . . . well, no matter. We shan't stop Petlyura. But he won't stay for long. And after him the Bolsheviks will come. That's why I shall go and fight. Against my will, but I shall fight! Because when we come face to face with them — then we shall see some fun. Either we shall bury them, or more likely, they will bury us. I drink to *that* meeting, gentlemen!

EVEN THE WISE CAN ERR
by Alexander Ostrovsky

Russian: Male

THE PLAY: A comedy of deception, *Even the Wise Can Err,* follows the intrigues of an ambitious writer who seeks to be included in the highest social circle in town. His machinations land him in the favors of his wealthy uncle, in the heart of his uncle's wife, and into an arranged marriage with the wealthiest and most eligible young woman around. If he had only kept his diary close to his heart, he would have never been discovered for the deceiver he is.

THE MONOLOGUE: Yegor Dmitrich Glumov (20s) has wheedled his way into the affections of all the right people and has taken copious notes on their ridiculous behaviors and habits. Unfortunately, his genius does not allow the possibility of his diary being found by his aunt. He has been found out and is unremorseful.

TIME AND PLACE: Moscow. 1860s. The garden of Glumov's uncle's manor.

Enter Glumov. Gorodulin respectfully hands him the diary.

GLUMOV: *(Taking the diary.)* Why quietly? I have no intention of either explaining or justifying my behavior. I only want to say that soon you yourselves will regret excluding me from your society.

(To Krutitsky.) Did you perceive that I was dishonest, Your Excellency? No doubt your penetrating mind discovered my dishonesty when I undertook to rewrite your treatise? — for surely no honest man would undertake such a task. Or perhaps you recognized my dishonesty when in your office I went into ecstasies over your most absurd phrases and grovelled like the meanest toady before you? Nothing of the sort. You were ready to kiss me for it, and if this miserable diary had not fallen into your hands you would have considered me an honest man for a long time to come.

(To Mamayev.) Or you, uncle — I suppose you, too, saw me for what I was? That time, perhaps, when you taught me to flatter Krutitsky? Or when you taught me to make love to your wife so as to distract her atten-

tion from other admirers; and I squirmed and simpered that I did not know how, that I was ashamed? You saw the pretense of it, but you said nothing; indeed it pleased you because it gave you an opportunity to spew out one of your homilies. I have long been cleverer than you and you know it, but when I pretend to be a simpleton and ask you for advice you are delighted and only too willing to declare me an honest man.

As for you, Sofia Ignatievna, I really did deceive you and therefore I owe you an apology — or rather not you, but Maria Ivanovna. I do not regret having deceived you. You pick up a tipsy peasant woman on the street and accept her ravings as a guide in choosing a husband for your niece. Who of the eligible young men does Manefa know? Who is she capable of recommending? Only the man who pays her the most money. Happily the man turned out to be me; he might have been an escaped criminal, and you would have given Masha to him just the same.

You have need of me, gentlemen. You cannot get on without men of my sort; if it is not me, it will be another. This other may be worse than me, and you will say: "Too bad, he cannot hold a candle to Glumov, but even so he is a good chap." *(To Krutitsky.)* You, Your Excellency, are considered a very gracious gentleman in society, but when you have a young man drawn up taut as a string in front of you in your office, humbly addressing you as Your Excellency and servilely agreeing with every word you say, you fairly wallow in the bliss of it. A really honest young man cannot hope to win your patronage, but such a one can count on having you rush about town to do him a favour.

I apologize, Your Excellency. *(To Mamayev.)* You need me too, uncle. Your servants refuse to listen to your sermons even for money, and I do it gratis.

And you, Ivan Ivanych — even you need me. To supply you with well-turned phrases for your speeches —And to help you write criticism.

And you need me, aunt.

You noticed nothing at all. It is only my diary that has incensed you. I don't know how it fell into your hands; even the wisest can err. But there is one thing I do know, gentlemen — so long as I circulated in your society, the only honest moments I knew were those in which I wrote this diary. No honest man could take any other view of you than that recorded in these pages. You raised my gorge. What did you find in my diary that offended you? What that you did not know already? You say the very same things about one another every day, only behind one another's back. If I had privately read to each one of you what I wrote about the others, you

would have applauded me. If anyone has a right to be angry and resentful, to rant and rage, it is me. I do not know who, but one of you honest people stole my diary. You have ruined me completely: deprived me of money and a good name. In driving me away you think you have got rid of me and there's an end to it. You think I will forgive you this. Do not deceive yourselves, ladies and gentlemen, you will pay heavily for it! I wish you good day. *(He goes out.)*
(Silence.)

THE GOVERNMENT INSPECTOR
by Nikolai Gogol

Russian: Male

THE PLAY: A classic Russian comedy, this play deals with the subject of mistaken identity and its comedic effects on an entire town. As was the way in pre-reform (1860s) Russia, the local town officials were subject to the constant oversight and intervention of officials higher up on the bureaucratic totem pole. In this play, word has spread that a government inspector will soon be arriving in town, and the corrupt officials go to all lengths to insure that they will not lose their jobs. What they don't know is what the inspector looks like, and thus the comedy of errors begins when an imposter comes to town and reaps the benefits of his mistaken identity.

THE MONOLOGUE: Ivan Alexandrovich Khlestakov (23) has found himself to be enjoying his position of Government Inspector. He delights in weaving tales of his majesty and importance, and occasionally gets a bit carried away with himself. In this monologue, he is building himself up in such a dramatic way as to make even the crowd around him swoon in admiration and fear of his greatness.

TIME AND PLACE: The Mayor's sitting room. The Mayor's house. A provincial Russian town. Late afternoon. 1860s.

KHLESTAKOV: I keep the best house in Petersburg. Everybody knows it. They call it Khlestakov House. (*Addressing everyone.*) Please, gentlemen, if you're ever in the capital, I urge you to visit me, by all means. I give parties, you know.

Words can't describe them! I'll have a watermelon on the table that sells for seven hundred rubles! A tureen of soup straight off the boat from Paris! You lift the lid, and the aroma — ah! There's nothing in the world to compare to it. I'm at a party every day of the week. We have our own card game: the foreign minister, the French ambassador, the German ambassador — and me. We play till we're exhausted. It's incredible! I'm barely able to drag myself up to my room on the fourth floor and say to the cook, "Hey, Mavrushka, take my coat." What am I blabbering about? I forgot, I live on the first floor. My staircase alone is worth . . . But you'd find my vestibule extremely interesting — counts and princes jostling each other, buzzing like bees — all you hear is bzz, bzz, bzz. Sometimes even a cabinet minister drops by . . . *(The Mayor and the others get up from their chairs, trembling.)* My letters are addressed, "Your Excellency." Once I even ran a ministry. Very curious — the director had vanished, nobody knew where. Well, naturally, there was a lot of talk. "How will we manage?" "Who will replace him?" The generals were keen on taking over, and some of them gave it a whirl. But the job was too much for them. What seemed easy enough turned out to be the damndest thing. They saw it was no use — they had to call on me. In a flash messengers came pouring down the streets, then more messengers, and more messengers . . . Think of it — thirty-five thousand messengers! "What's the problem," I asked. "Ivan Alexandrovich Khlestakov! Come! Take charge!" I confess, I was a bit taken aback. I came out in my robe, meaning to turn them down. But I thought to myself, the tsar will hear of it, and there's my service record to worry about . . . "All right, gentlemen, I accept. Very well," I said, "I accept. Only I won't stand for any nonsense. No, sir! I'm always on my toes! I'm the sort who . . ." And that's exactly the way it turned out. When I made my rounds of the ministry, you'd have thought an earthquake had struck — everyone quivering, shaking like a leaf. *(Mayor and others tremble in terror. Khlestakov is carried away.)* Oh! I'm not one to play games! I put the fear of God into every last one of them! Even the cabinet is scared stiff of me. And why not, I ask you? That's how I'm made! No one gets in my way. I tell one and all — I know who I am. I'm everywhere! Everywhere! I pop in and out of the palace. Tomorrow they're promoting me to field marshal! *(Slips and almost falls to the floor. The officials support him differentially.)*

MARRIAGE
by Nikolai Gogol

Russian: Male

THE PLAY: Described by the author as "a completely unlikely incident in two acts," *Marriage* is a comic look at the old tradition of matchmaking. Fyokla is the town's local matchmaker, and she is preparing to get a husband for the beautiful, young Agafya. On her list of potential mates is the confirmed and stubborn bachelor, Podkolyosin. With the added intrusion of Podkolyosin's friend Kochkaryov, and the roomful of eager suitors, Fyokla has her hands full. The happy ending is quite possibly what the author meant by "unlikely."

THE MONOLOGUE: Podkolyosin (20s) has been pressured into believing that he loves the idea of marriage and a wife, especially if she is as wonderful as Agafya. Before he even knew what happened, he became engaged and is waiting in her room to be taken to the church for his wedding. This has all happened within a matter of hours. As he waits for her to come down for their wedding, he begins to have second thoughts.

TIME AND PLACE: Agafya's room, in her house behind the dressmaker's house, in back of the beer hall. A small town in Russia near a bigger town in Russia. Anytime.

PODKOLYOSIN: Yes indeed, what have I been, until this moment? Have I grasped the essence of life? No. I haven't grasped a thing. How dull I've been . . . done nothing, good-for-nothing. I merely existed . . . went to my office, had dinner, slept — in other words I've been the most boring, mundane man on earth. Yes indeed, the man who refuses to marry is a fool, and there are many such blind fools. If I were the Tsar, I'd order every bachelor to marry immediately — there wouldn't be an unmarried man left in the whole country! When one considers . . . that one will be married in a matter of hours . . . minutes . . . in a matter of minutes one will taste the ecstasy that is the stuff of fairy tales . . .. a joy which no words can express . . . *(A pause.)* On the other hand . . . it's odd, when one takes the time to consider . . . binding oneself for life . . . all those years. And afterward, no retreat, no turning back — you can't run away. The supper's ready, everything's prepared. And really, it would be impossible to escape — there are people at all the doors, watching — I can't — no, I mustn't — but here's an open window. No, no, I would never — it's so . . . undignified. And besides, it's too high up — *(He crosses to the window.)* Well, it's not really so high. Just one story, as a matter of fact. No — and I don't have my hat. How could I leave without my hat? It's unheard of. On the other hand, if I can't leave with my hat . . . I ought to try to leave without it . . . eh? I might try . . . *(And he climbs onto the window ledge.)* Heavens, what a height! *(And he jumps.)* Looord deliver meeee!

MORE SINNED AGAINST THAN SINNING
by Alexander Ostrovsky

Russian: Male

THE PLAY: When Lubov Otradina's love deserts her for a wealthier, more socially positioned woman and leaves her with a young son who dies that very day, Lubov leaves town, changes her name, and begins a new life. After seventeen years she returns to her town as a famous actress. Unbeknownst to her, another young actor in her company, Grigory Neznamov, is actually her long-lost "dead" son. He did not die and has been living as an orphan/foster child. In a twist of fate he joins the theater as their newest, young male lead, and the family is reunited during a benefit run of a play in their old hometown.

THE MONOLOGUE: Grigory Neznamov (22 to 23) has been asked to visit the celebrity actress Kruchinina in her hotel suite. He and his friend, Shmaga, wait for her and are prepared to hate her. When she comes to them, though, Neznamov is charmed and feels more natural compassion and love for her in an instant than he can explain. He reveals his background and the shame he bears because of it to this new acquaintance.

TIME AND PLACE: Kruchinina's sitting room of her hotel suite. A large provincial town.

NEZNAMOV: Hear? Even he thinks he can make fun of me. And so he can. Who am I? Nobody. Less than nobody. He's an individual, a social unit, he has a name, he owns a passport. In this passport you will read: "Son of a retired office clerk; expelled from school for bad behaviour; employed as a copy clerk in the Orphans' Court and dismissed for indolence; taken to court for being implicated in the theft of a woolen greatcoat and released under suspicion." There's a document for you! Who wouldn't be delighted to own it! Gives a man a clean slate. He can look anyone straight in the eye, tell anyone exactly who he is. Is it any satisfaction to me that, thanks to you, I can stay in this infernal town? The theater has been trying to get rid of me for a long time and soon it will. What will become of me then — a tramp without kith or kin or a worthy occupation? Where am I to live? No town will have me — or rather, any town will, but only at the expense of the state; in other words, locked up. I'm not a thief and have never had the slightest inclination to be one; I'm not a highwayman or a murderer; I'm not ruled by bloody instincts. Yet I have a premonition that, willy-nilly, I will end up in jail. People like me had best be left alone; doing them favours only makes them angrier.

Take you and me, for instance: what are you to me? Absolutely nothing. I don't give a snap of my fingers whether you live or die; as strangers each of us should go his own way without thought of the other. And here you are forcing your patronage on me and expecting me to be grateful for it. Well, rest assured I shall not thank you for it. Even so my friends will give me no peace; at every opportunity they will throw it in my face: "If it wasn't for Kruchinina you wouldn't be here." "If it wasn't for Kruchinina you'd be footing it by now." On and on until I'd come to hate you, and I don't want to do that. I want to remain indifferent to you. I realize how tempting it is to be magnanimous, especially when everyone flatters you and grants your every wish, but you can't always count on being thanked for your goodness; sometimes you must expect to have to pay for it.

MORE SINNED AGAINST THAN SINNING
by Alexander Ostrovsky

Russian: Male

THE PLAY: When Lubov Otradina's love deserts her for a wealthier, more so-cially positioned woman and leaves her with a young son who dies that very day, Lubov leaves town, changes her name, and begins a new life. After seventeen years she returns to her town as a famous actress. Unbeknownst to her, another young actor in her company, Grigory Neznamov, is actually her long-lost "dead" son. He did not die and has been living as an orphan/foster child. In a twist of fate he joins the theater as their newest, young male lead, and the family is reunited during a ben-efit run of a play in their old hometown.

THE MONOLOGUE: Grigory Neznamov (22 to 23) has developed a reputation amongst his castmates as being a bit of a troublemaker. Still unwitting that he is in the presence of his real mother, he is invited to dinner where it is hoped that he will get drunk and embarrass himself and the leading lady. After hearing rumors about her past and the scandals that plagued her early in her career, Neznamov makes a toast designed to wound her to the heart.

TIME AND PLACE: A moonlit night. A garden terrace of a large house. A large provincial town.

NEZNAMOV: Ladies and gentlemen, I propose a toast to mothers who abandon their children!
    May they know nothing but joy and happiness, and may their paths be strewn with lilies and roses. Let nothing and nobody cast a shadow upon their sunny existence. Let nothing and nobody remind them of the bitter lot of their unfortunate children. Why should their peace of mind be disturbed? They have done all they could for their offspring — wept over them, kissed them more or less tenderly, and bid them farewell: "Live, my darling, as best you can, but better it would be if you died." The truth is the truth, and there's no denying it: for those newcomers into this world death is the best thing that could happen to them. Not all of them are granted this happiness, however. (*He bows his head and reflects for a*

moment.) Some of these mothers are sentimental; it is not enough for them to kiss their babes and shed a few tears over them; they must hang trinkets round their necks to be remembered by. Who, pray, is the child to remember? And why should he remember? Why should he be constantly reminded of his shame and misery? There are plenty of people who are only too glad to remind him he is a foundling, that his origins trace back to a doorstep. If those mothers only knew how many tears their children shed upon such trinkets, how desperately they implore the unfeeling gold to give up its secret! "Who hung you here?" they cry, "Where are you now? Why don't you come at my call? Cannot you spare a single tear to ease my suffering?" Oh, how these trinkets sear the breasts of those who wear them!

THE SEAGULL
by Anton Chekhov

Russian: Male

THE PLAY: Chekhov's classic play about the lives and loves of a theatrical family and the havoc that the pursuit of art wreaks on their relationships with each other is not traditionally done in a Russian dialect, but the poetry and imagery of the text will be useful for the actor to explore.

THE MONOLOGUE: As the artists gather at his mother's house for a performance of his new play, Treplov (25) shares his insecurities and feelings of inadequacy with his uncle Sorin.

TIME AND PLACE: Sorin's country estate. Evening. Outside on the terrace.

TREPLEV: Already she's in a "state," because here upon this pathetic little stage it will be Nina's hour, not hers. *(Looks at his watch.)* A psychological wonder — that's my mother. Unquestionably talented, brilliant, capable of falling to pieces over a book she's reading, of rattling off all of Nekrasov by heart, of nursing the sick like an angel — but just try mentioning the name of Duse in her presence, and "oh-ho"! No, we must sing her praise and hers alone — yes, sing it, write it, shout it — wild, ecstatic praise over her stunning performance in *La Dame Aux Camélias* or God knows what play. But here, in the country, where you can't get that drug for her, she gets bored and evil-tempered, and all of us — we are her enemies, everything's our fault. And she gets so superstitious — she's afraid of these candles burning or whether it's the thirteenth day of the month. And stingy? She has 70,000 rubles in the bank in Odessa, that I know for a fact. But ask her to lend you anything, and she bursts into tears.

[SORIN: You've gotten it into that head of yours that your mother doesn't like your play, and you're all worked up in advance, that's all. Calm down, your mother adores you.]

TREPLEV: *(Plucking petals off a flower.)* She loves me, she loves me not; she loves me, she loves me not; she loves me, she loves me not. *(Laughs.)* You see, my mother doesn't love me. And why should she? She wants romance and adventure, a whole new life for herself, a gay, romantic life, and here I am, twenty-five years old, a constant reminder that she's not so young any more. When I'm not around, she's only thirty-two, and when I am, presto! — she's forty-three, and she hates me for it. She also knows I don't believe in the "'theater," such as it is. She adores the theater — she thinks she's serving mankind and her sacred art, but if you ask me, our theater of today is dull and narrow-minded. Every evening, when the curtain goes up, and there under the bright lights, in a room with three walls, those celebrated artists, those high priests of our sacred art, when they play it all out before us, how we mortals eat, and drink, and love, and go around wearing our clothes and leading our lives; when out of this vulgar scenario we are served up some kind of message or moral, however meagre, ready for our daily domestic consumption; when after its one thousandth incarnation all these plays seem to me to be the same, time after time after time the same, then I flee — I flee like Maupassant fled the Eiffel Tower, because it outraged him how enormously trite it was.

[SORIN: Without the theater, nothing is possible.]

TREPLEV: We need new forms. We must have new forms, and if we don't we might as well have nothing at all. *(Looks at his watch.)* I love my mother. I love her very much, but she leads a chaotic life, forever carrying on with that novelist, her name all over the papers — and I've had it with her. Although sometimes I think it's my own mortal ego; I feel sorry for myself that I have a famous actress for a mother, and if only she were an ordinary woman, oh, how happy I would be. Uncle, can you imagine a more desperate and pathetic situation: Here she is, holding court in her own home, surrounded by all sorts of artists and writers, and there, in the midst of all these luminaries sits the only nobody — me, And why do they tolerate me, because I am her son. And who am I? What am I? I left the university in my third year, due, as they say, to "circumstances beyond one's control," or whatever the phrase is — with no talent, no money, and a passport announcing, loud and clear, that I am a member of the Kiev bourgeoisie. Yes, indeed, my father was a true member of the Kiev bourgeoisie, although he also happened to have been a well-known actor. And thus, it came to pass, when in my mother's living room, all these artists and writers bestowed upon me their benevolent attention, it dawned on me that what they really were doing was sizing me up in all my insignificance. I could read their minds and how I suffered from the humiliation.

THE SHADOW
by Evgeny Shvarts

Russian: Male

THE PLAY: Set in a fictional time and place, this play has been described as "a satire, an ode, and, perhaps, even partly a fable." (From the introduction to the play in *An Anthology of Russian Plays*, edited, translated, and introduced by F. D. Reeve. The quote is attributed to Lidiya Chukovskaya.) A Scholar, eager to experience the adventures of his idol, Hans Christian Andersen, ventures to the same place he did and encounters an odd group of people. It is a country where the fairy tales are reality, and logic makes no sense. The Scholar soon loses his Shadow and spends the rest of the play trying to get everything to end up happily ever after.

THE MONOLOGUE: At the top of the play, The Scholar (26) sets the tone for the rest of the adventure to come in this metaphor about the way we see things.

TIME AND PLACE: A southern country. A hotel room. Anytime. Anyplace.

A small room in a hotel in a southern country. There are two doors — one into the corridor, the other onto a balcony. It is twilight. The Scholar is half reclining on a sofa, a young man of twenty-six. He is fumbling around on the table with his hand — looking for his glasses.

SCHOLAR: When you lose your glasses, it's, of course, unpleasant. But at the same time it's wonderful, too — in the twilight, my whole room seems different from usual. This plaid blanket, thrown over the armchair, now seems to me a very sweet and kind princess. I'm in love with her, and she's come to visit me. She's not alone, of course. A princess isn't supposed to go around without a retinue. This tall, skinny clock in its wooden case isn't a clock at all. It's the princess' eternal companion, the privy councillor. His heart pounds regularly like a pendulum, his counsels change in accordance with the requirements of the time, and he gives them in a whisper. It's not for nothing, of course, that he's privy. And if the counsels of the privy councillor turn out to be ruinous, he later repudiates them completely. He insists that people simply didn't catch what he said, and that's very practical of him. But who's this? Who's this stranger, thin and slender, all in black with a white face? Why do I suddenly have the idea that that's the princess' fiancé? Now, you now, it's me who's in love with the princess! I'm so much in love with her that it will be simply monstrous if she marries somebody else. *(Laughs.)* The charm of these fancies is that I'll have no sooner put my glasses on when everything will be back in place. The blanket will be a blanket, the clock a clock, and this sinister stranger will vanish. *(Rummages around on the table with his hands.)* Now, here are my glasses. *(Puts on his glasses and shrieks.)* What's this?

SECTION FOUR

AMERICAN

(New York)

AMERICAN (NEW YORK)
INTRODUCTION

In dialects class, the accent that brings out the most energy, enthusiasm, and bold character choices from the actors is the New York accent. Although some may argue that there is no New York dialect any more, there are definite region-specific patterns and sound changes that color the speech of the lifelong New York area resident. These speech qualities, coupled with the physical character and energy of the New York native, make for wonderfully new, typically assertive, good choices in acting classes. Quiet people find a reason to be loud, physically restrained people find an excuse to be more expressive, and people who tend to go for the easiest, stereotypical choice are encouraged to move beyond that into a less common, deeper option. Students love playing with a New York accent!

As with most major metropolitan areas, New York City is home to an eclectic group of accents and speech patterns. When playing a character from a tough, bustling American city, the most frequently used accent is a general New York accent, most closely equated to the borough of Brooklyn. For our purposes, scenes in this section represent the various districts of New York, Long Island, and New Jersey.

New York, traditionally, is and has been home to many different ethnic groups and social classes. Because of its proximity to Ellis Island, the population of New York in the early days was a broad mix of new arrivals. Neighborhoods formed where people clustered in groups based on a shared language, history, and culture. This same segregation still exists today; one can find a neighborhood for every culture and ethnicity.

The accents of New Yorkers, therefore, are not necessarily uniform to all New York inhabitants. The actor who is undertaking a Brooklyn accent must research the nationality and upbringing of his or her character to figure out which flavor of the Brooklyn accent will be most appropriate. Although there are some consistent sound changes, each ethnic/borough group will offer its own unique pronunciation or inflection pattern. Simply put, an Italian Brooklyn accent sounds different from a Jewish Brooklyn accent, which sounds different from an Italian Bronx accent and so forth.

It is important to remember that the New York accents evolved from a culture of working-class, recently immigrated, usually undereducated, expressive people. Although the corporate world of today tends to breed a general, common American speech, and it is more difficult to find a thick New York accent in the population of the upwardly mobile working class, the New York accent in all its variations does still exist.

To remain truthful and nonstereotypical, the actor must keep it simple when applying the New York accent to the character at hand. For the New York sounds/patterns, less is more.

- Owing in part to the tradition of being a blue-collar laboring community, there is a toughness or roughness in the delivery of the New York accent . . . completely bold.
- The native languages of the speaker and his or her relatives will determine the exact sound of the New York accent.
- Stereotypical, but still quite prevalent, is the inordinate amount of swearing among New Yorkers. The swearing, however, is not as loaded as it is for people in other regions. Swearing to a New Yorker is almost like a verbal pause of thought (much the way Californians say "like" all the time.) Of course, the actor will only swear if the script says to swear, and it may not be necessary to make the swear word the operative of the line—it may not be important.
- New Yorkers, due to the rushed pace of city living and overcrowding, speak quickly with little room for anyone to interrupt them.
- People from New York deliver their words without fear — they are totally unafraid to voice their opinions. A friend from Brooklyn reports that you always know who your enemies and who your friends are in Brooklyn — no one puts on the false pretense of being kind to your face and then talks bad about you when you're gone. They tell you to your face if they don't like you or what you said, and if you've got a problem with it, well, "that's *your* problem!"
- The volume of the accent tends to be slightly higher than average.
- Without sacrificing the intelligibility of your words for the audience, the dialect can be less articulate and a little mumbly.
- The dialect tends to resonate (depending on the ethnicity of the speaker) in the sinuses, throat, and/or chest.
- New Yorkers are unapologetic in their carriage and speech.

New York Film, Television, and Audio References

FILMS

Mickey Blue Eyes (Italian)	James Caan, Cast
Summer of Sam (Italian/Latino)	John Leguizamo, Cast
Analyze This (Italian)	Robert DeNiro, Cast
Donnie Brasco (Italian)	Al Pacino, Johnny Depp
Smoke, Blue in the Face (Italian)	Harvey Keitel
Moonstruck (Italian)	Cast
Prizzi's Honor (Italian)	Angelica Huston, Cast
Goodfellas, My Cousin Vinny (Italian)	Joe Pesci
My Cousin Vinny (Italian)	Marisa Tomei
Goodfellas (Italian)	Lorraine Bracco
Godfather I, II, III (Italian)	Cast
Saturday Night Fever, Grease (Italian)	John Travolta
Serpico (Italian)	Al Pacino
Raging Bull (Italian)	Robert DeNiro, Cathy Moriarty
Taxi Driver (Italian)	Robert DeNiro
The In-Laws, Grosse Point Blank (Jewish)	Alan Arkin
Funny Girl (Jewish)	Barbra Streisand
And Justice For All (Jewish)	Lee Strasberg
Quiz Show (Jewish)	John Turturro
Torch Song Trilogy (Jewish)	Harvey Fierstein
Using People (Yiddish)	Cast
Brighton Beach Memoirs, *Broadway Bound* (Jewish)	Cast
Cemetery Club (Yiddish)	Cast
White Men Can't Jump (Bronx, Latina)	Rosie Perez
Spic-O-Rama, Mambo Mouth (Latino)	John Leguizamo
Hangin with the Homeboys (Varied)	Cast
Crooklyn (African-American)	Cast

TELEVISION

"All in the Family" (Bronx)	"Taxi"
"Laverne and Shirley"	"Welcome Back Kotter"
"The Nanny"	"Who's the Boss"
"Seinfeld"	

DIALECT TAPES AND BOOKS

Stage Dialects	Jerry Blunt
Dialects for the Stage	Evangeline Machlin
Acting with an Accent — NYC	David Alan Stern

NEW YORK SOUNDS

- Keep in mind that the following vowel changes represent a general New York sound; some characters may require a more specifically placed sound.

a → a/eyuh (nasalized)	Al, sand, can → eyuhl, seyuhnd, ceyuhn
ah → oowa (rounder)	all, daughters → oowall, doowatuhz
oo → uhoo	two, new shoe → tuhoo, nuhoo, shuhoo
ow → aoh (sharper)	how, cow, now → haoh, caoh, naoh

- The wuestion of *r* — the *r* sound is dropped at the ends of words and before consonants. If the *r* appears at the end of a word and the next word starts with a vowel, you would say the *r* sound (car and driver).

ear → ee uh	here, near, we're → hee uh, nee uh, wee uh
air → ehyuh	pears, there, where → pehyuhz, thehyuh, whehyuh
oor → oo wuh	sure, pure, poor → shoo wuh, pyoo wuh, poo wuh
are → ah	cart, far, large → caht, fah, lahge

- Other consonant changes:

[t] [d] → [t$_h$] [d$_h$] top, don't, tan → t$_h$op, d$_h$on't, t$_h$an
(air splashes off these as you make them against your top teeth)
[h] → [y] huge, humid, human → yuge, yumid, yuman
(dropped at the beginnings of words)
[t] → [d] better, butter, put it over → bedduh, budduh, pud id ovuh
(between vowels)

- Other consonant changes:

[g] going, coming → goin', comin'
(dropped on -ing endings)
[ing] + [g] singer, Long Island, ringing → sing guh, lawng gisland, ring gin
(with some speakers)
[th] → [d] this, them, those → dhis, dhem, dhose
[th] → [t] with, think, thanks → wit, tink, tanks

NEW YORK PRACTICE SENTENCES

a → a or eyuh:
Angela and Andrew can't stand Candace. Can Anne dance with half the band?

ow → aoh:
How does the cow go around the clown? The crown fell on the brown ground.

ah → oowa:
My daughter Dawn loves to talk to dogs about coffee and wall-to-wall carpet.

oo → uhoo:
Two youths in the pool. The glue is for Blue Tooth, the goon.

ear → ee uh:
Get over here! I have no fear of the deer. Here is near the Lear jet.

air → ehyuh:
Where was the care for the bare bear on the stairs? I dare you to stare there.

oor → oo wuh:
The poor pure loser was sure new to the sewer. The poor doer was newer than the boor.

are → ah:
The car is far from the park. Dark is hard to part from stark.

[t] [d] → [t$_h$] [d$_h$]:
Don't tell Darcy about Tony and Terri. Take that doughnut down to Dawn.

[h] → [y]:
Huge humid clouds settled down on the humans.

[t] → [d]:

The better the butter, the better the batter. The pretty little petal was metal.

[ing + g]:

I was singing and thinking that I could sing all day. Long Island is ringing

.

[th] → [d]:

Without these things, this would not get done.

[th] → [t]:

Think about it, thanks aren't thoughtful unless they're thankful.

BOYS' LIFE
by Howard Korder

American (New York): Female

THE PLAY: Through a series of vignettes, the angst of relationships and the passing of time is revealed in the lives of urbanites in their late 20s.

THE MONOLOGUE: Lisa (25 to 29) has just found another woman's panties in her boyfriend Don's bed. As he tries to apologize and explain that he really feels bad about it and that he truly loves her, Lisa lets him know what is important to her in a relationship.

TIME AND PLACE: The present. Later evening. Don's bedroom. A big city.

LISA: I *heard* what you said! You love me! That doesn't mean shit! This isn't high school. I'm wearing your *pin*. You want me to tell you what really counts? Out here with the graduates?

It's not worth it! Do what you want, it doesn't matter to me. I don't even know you, Don. After four months I don't know who you are or why you do what you do. You keep getting your dick stuck in things. What is that all about, anyway? Will someone please explain that to me? *(Pause.)* Don't look at me that way.

Like a whipped dog. It's just pathetic.

Do you have any idea what you're saying?

I'm sorry, but "I feel bad" isn't even in the running. Not at all. We're talking about faith. *Semper fidelis,* like the marines. They don't leave people lying in foxholes. They just do it. They don't "feel bad."

(Pause.) You don't understand what I'm talking about, do you? You're just afraid of being punished. I'm not your *mother.* I don't spank. *(Pause.)* I'm going. Have fun fucking your bargain shopper and cracking jokes with your creepy friends.

BRIGHTON BEACH MEMOIRS
by Neil Simon

American (New York): Female

THE PLAY: The first of Mr. Simon's famous and popular memoir trilogy (followed by *Biloxi Blues* and *Broadway Bound*), in *Brighton Beach Memoirs* we are introduced to the rich and fascinating characters in the life of aspiring writer, Eugene Jerome. The extended Jerome family is large and crowded into a single-family wooden frame house in Brighton Beach. Eugene Jerome records not only his puberty and burgeoning interest in things beyond baseball, but also observes and records the dramas (large and small) that occur in the lives of his mother, aunt, father, brother, and cousins as they live out one week in September 1937.

THE MONOLOGUE: Nora Morton (16) is Eugene's cousin. She has just come home from her dance class with some amazing news. She can hardly contain herself as she gathers up her family in the living room to reveal her fabulous good fortune.

TIME AND PLACE: Living room of the Jerome house. Brighton Beach, Brooklyn, New York. 6:30 PM. September 1937.

NORA: Sit down, Mom, because I don't want you fainting on the floor.
You too, Aunt Kate. Okay. Is everybody ready?
(A little breathless.) Okay! Here goes! . . . I'm going to be in a Broadway show! *(They look at her in a stunned silence.)* It's a musical called *Abracadabra* . . . This man, Mr. Beckman, he's a producer, came to our dancing class this afternoon and he picked out three girls. We have to be at the Hudson Theater on Monday morning at ten o'clock to audition for the dance director. But on the way out he took me aside and said the job was good as mine. I have to call him tomorrow. I may have to go to into town to talk to him about it. They start rehearsing a week from Monday and then it goes to Philadelphia, Wilmington and Washington . . . and then it comes to New York the second week of December. There are nine big musical numbers and there's going to be a big tank on the stage that you can see through and the big finale all takes place with the entire cast all under water . . . I mean, can you believe it? I'm going to be in a Broadway show, Momma! *(They are all still stunned.)*

BRIGHTON BEACH MEMOIRS
by Neil Simon

American (New York): Female

THE PLAY: The first of Mr. Simon's famous and popular memoir trilogy (followed by *Biloxi Blues* and *Broadway Bound*), in *Brighton Beach Memoirs* we are introduced to the rich and fascinating characters in the life of aspiring writer, Eugene Jerome. The extended Jerome family is large and crowded into a single-family wooden frame house in Brighton Beach. Eugene Jerome records not only his puberty and burgeoning interest in things beyond baseball, but also observes and records the dramas (large and small) that occur in the lives of his mother, aunt, father, brother, and cousins as they live out one week in September 1937.

THE MONOLOGUE: Nora Morton (16) is Eugene's cousin. The pressure of living so tightly knit to her relatives is beginning to wear on her. After revealing that she has a great opportunity to be in a Broadway show, she is told by her mother that her fate lies in the answer of her Uncle Jack. If he says she can audition for the show, then she can. Protesting that Uncle Jack is not her father, Nora finds that she has no say in the matter and must obey her mother's final word. She storms off to her quarter of the room she splits with her sister and her cousins Eugene and Stanley. As her sister tries to comfort her, Nora remembers her father.

TIME AND PLACE: Living room of the Jerome house. Brighton Beach, Brooklyn, New York. 6:30 PM. September 1937.

NORA: Mostly I remember his pockets.

   When I was six or seven he always brought me home a little surprise. Like a Hershey or a top. He'd tell me to get it in his coat pocket. So I'd run to the closet and put my hand in and it felt as big as a tent. I wanted to crawl in there and go to sleep. And there were all these terrific things in there, like Juicy Fruit gum or Spearmint Life Savers and bits of cellophane and crumbled pieces of tobacco and movie stubs and nickels and pennies and rubber bands and paper clips and his grey suede gloves that he wore in the winter time.

Then I found his coat in Mom's closet and I put my hand in the pocket. And everything was gone. It was emptied and dry cleaned and it felt cold . . . And that's when I knew he was really dead. *(Thinks a moment.)* Oh God, I wish we had our own place to live. I hate being a boarder. Listen, let's make a pact . . . The first one who makes enough money promises not to spend any on herself, but saves it all to get a house for you and me and Mom. That means every penny we get from now on, we save for the house . . . We can't buy *anything*. No lipstick or magazines or nail polish or bubble gum. *Nothing* . . . Is it a pact?

DEAD END
by Sidney Kingsley

American (New York): Female

THE PLAY: A classic, gritty American realism play, *Dead End* paints the portrait of a New York neighborhood in the midst of gentrification. The poor, dirty neighborhood regulars find themselves with new neighbors — the wealthy residents of a private new apartment complex (The East River Terrace Apartments). As the boys of the neighborhood swim in the murky, polluted East River, their wealthy neighbors are treated to an indoor pool and all the best amenities. The friction between the haves and the have-nots builds throughout the play, erupting in a final tragic ending.

THE MONOLOGUE: Kay (20s) is living the high life in East River Terrace Apartments, but she comes from a much lower situation. She lives with a man almost twice her age who keeps her in the lifestyle she desires. But her heart belongs to Gimpty. She is preparing to leave on a sailing voyage with her live-in partner and tries to explain to Gimpty why she had to choose the way she did.

TIME AND PLACE: 1935. A dead end of a New York street, ending in a wharf over the East River, near the East Fifties. Night.

KAY: This isn't the miracle we were looking for.

How long would it last us? Perhaps a year, then what? I've been through all that. I couldn't go through it again.

(*Softly, trying to make him see the picture realistically, reasonably.*) It's not all selfishness, Pete. I'm thinking of you too. I could do this. I could go and live with you and be happy — (*And she means it.*) — and then when poverty comes . . . and we begin to torture each other, what would happen? I'd leave you and go back to Jack. He needs me too, you see, I'm pretty certain of him, but what would become of you then? That sound pretty bitchy, I suppose.

It's just that we can't have everything . . . ever. (*She rises.*)

Good-bye, darling.

(*One sob escaping her.*) Oh, Pete, forgive me if I've hurt you. Please forgive me!

GIRL GONE
by Jacquelyn Reingold

American (New York): Female

THE PLAY: A topless dancer has lost her best friend to a senseless and unexplained murder. Her love and confusion surrounding her feelings for her friend are disguised by her unflagging desire to find out what happened to her friend and to solve the mystery of her death. Soon, her quest takes over her life, and she finds herself living the life of her friend to retrace the final events of her friend's life. She wears her clothes, dates her old boyfriends, and comes to a disturbing and heart-rending conclusion.

THE MONOLOGUE: Tish (21 to 24) is trying to deal with the grief of losing her best friend. Near the beginning of the play, her thoughts are still a bit muddled and she attempts to figure them out.

TIME AND PLACE: Dressing room of a topless bar. The present. A city.

Lights dim on dancers.

TISH: *(To the audience.)* Sometimes you open the door. You think who could it be, it's the door, they knock, they ring, you open it. Sometimes they lie and say they are who they aren't. Sometimes they have uniforms, they dress like deliverymen firemen policemen exterminators, someone you thought you knew, might have loved. Sometimes the elevator opens, and as you fall down the shaft you wonder what happened and why you didn't see.

Sometimes you reach for the shampoo, but someone left the Nair there and you can't figure out why your hair's all gone. Or for your birthday someone leaves a present at the door, it's a thousand piece jigsaw puzzle — with no picture on the cover of the box. And then for Christmas you get a box with a pretty picture — and inside — a thousand pieces each from a different puzzle. Sometimes you wake up and think you got it figured out, the next day you realize it's just your figure that's out — big is back, small is in, your clothes just don't fit; your best friend went away so you're left with pieces that don't match, walking down the street looking for cracks. She was my friend. It's different when it's your friend. It's not like channel 5, page 3, 88 on your AM dial. She was. My friend. I. See. She used to do my makeup. We used to talk. And now I forgot. I. Right arm out. Left foot. Left arm. I forgot how to dance. I lost my friend. Her name was Jean. She changed my life. She taught me how to dance. "It's like ducks," she said. *(To audience.)* I'm watching you and you're watching me, and I'm wondering if you killed my best friend.

A HATFUL OF RAIN
by Michael Gazzo

American (New York): Female

THE PLAY: A dramatic look at the life of a young man and the effects of drug addiction. Set in a New York tenement apartment, the story follows the troubles of Johnny, a young Army vet who was wounded during his tour of service and became addicted to the drugs he was given in the hospital. As he tries to take care of his wife and the baby on the way, he tries just as desperately to keep his addiction a secret.

THE MONOLOGUE: Celia (20 to 22) has found a closer companionship with her brother-in-law as her husband continues to act mysteriously. She reveals the hidden frustration she feels at her job to her brother-in-law, Polo, and they begin along the dangerous path of "too much closeness."

TIME AND PLACE: 1950s. An apartment living room/kitchen area in New York's Lower East Side. Early evening.

CELIA: *(Taking off stocking.)* All right smarty, forget it. — The Union Metal Company of America — that's where you should work, Polo. At least there's a little excitement at your job — Do you know that when I started working in the carpeted air-conditioned desert I could take dictation at the rate of 120 words a minute. I could type 90 words — Today I was sitting at my desk pretending to be busy. I have papers in all the drawers. I keep shuffling them from drawer to drawer. I break pencils and sharpen them. Mr. Wagner called me in his office today and I bustled in with my steno pad — and you know what he called me in for? He wanted to know. Was I happy? Was Union Metals treating me right. I've been there five years come Ash Wednesday — and every six months they call you in and ask you the same thing — Are you happy? *(Goes to bureau, gets hanger, and crosses to sink. Puts hanger on table as she passes.)* *(Starts to rinse stockings.)* Nobody ever quits Union Metals — and no one ever gets fired. A bonus on Christmas, a turkey on Thanksgiving, long holiday weekends. They've insured Johnny and I against sickness, and the plague, everything for the employees — boat rides, picnics, sick leave, a triple savings interest account, the vacations keep getting longer, we have a doctor, a nurse, and a cafeteria, four coffee breaks a day, if it gets too hot they send you home, and if it rains it's perfectly all right if you're late — and it's the dullest job in the whole world. *(Hangs stockings on hanger which he is holding.)* I got another raise today — *(There is a pause and they look at each other. She crosses to bed for robe.)*

THE MINEOLA TWINS
by Paula Vogel

American (New York): Female

THE PLAY: Described by the author as "a comedy in seven scenes, four dreams and five wigs," *The Mineola Twins* follows the life paths of identical twins from age 17 to 47. The twins could not be any more opposite, much to their consternation, and their sons seem to have been born to the wrong mother (Myra's son is more like Myrna and vice versa). The historical time periods serve as both a backdrop and an inspiration for the attitudes and actions of the main characters.

THE MONOLOGUE: In this dream-sequence monologue, Myra (17) describes many of the nightmarish images of the time, coupled with her own impressions.

TIME AND PLACE: Mineola, Long Island. 1959.

NOTE: Dream-sequence monologues need not be played any differently than a normal conversation one would have a scene partner. Consider the audience your scene partner.

Eerie lighting. Myra Richards, age seventeen, stands in a trance, in a letter sweater with several Ms stitched on askew; it looks like bloody hands have clutched and stretched the knit during an apocalyptic Sock Hop that ended in disaster. Spooky 1950s sci-fi movie music. The Voice comments to us:

[VOICE: Dream Sequence Number One. Myra In Homeroom. Myra In Hell.]
A flash of lightning. A crackle of thunder.
MYRA: So. It was like homeroom, only we were calculating the hypotenuse of hygiene. I whispered to Billy Bonnell — what does that mean? And he said: Yuck-yuck — it's the same angle as the triangle under your skirt, Myra Richards. Yuck-yuck.

Shut-Up Creep! Thhwwack! My metal straight edge took off the top of his cranium. And then Mrs. Hopkins said, in this voice from the crypt: Miss Richards — what is the hypotenuse of hygiene?

And just as I was saying Excuse Me, Mrs. Hopkins, But I Didn't Know What the Homework Was for Today on Account of Being Suspended Last Week By You 'Cause of the Dumb-Ass Dress Code — [VOICE: *(Cuts in on the intercom:)* " . . . Get . . . To . . . The . . . Door . . .Now."]

And the Nuclear Air Raid Siren Came On, Real Loud. And kids started bawling and scrambling under their desks. Somehow we knew it was For Real. We could hear this weird whistling of the bombs coming for us, with a straight line drawn from Moscow to Mineola. Dead Center for the Nassau County Court House. Dead Center for Roosevelt Field. And Dead Center for Mineola High. Home of the Mineola Mustangs.

And I knew it would do diddly-squat to get under the desk. Something drew me into the hall, where there was pulsing Red Light and Green Smoke.

Like Christmas in Hell.

I just kept walking.

Kids' bodies were mangled everywhere. In the middle of the hall, Our Principal Mr. Chotner was hypotenusing under Miss Dorothy Comby's skirt.

I just kept walking.

The girls' Glee Club had spread-eagled Mr. Koch the driver's ed instructor further down the hall, and they were getting the long-handled custodian's broom out of the closet.

I just kept walking.

I checked my watch. Five minutes to the Apocalypse. I could hear the bombs humming louder now. I thought of crossing against the lights and getting home. But there's nothing lonelier than watching your parents hug while you curl up on the rug alone and Mom's ceramic dogs melt on the mantle as the sky glows its final Big Red.

Then I heard The Voice on the intercom say to me
[VOICE: . . . Find . . . Her.]

I had to Obey The Voice.

I knew that at the bottom of the stairwell, I would find my twin sister Myrna, hiding from me. Curled up in a little O, her back to me. Just like Old Times in the Womb. *(The Voice begins to breathe rapidly into the microphone.)*

I entered the stairwell at the top. The lights were out. The air was thick. The stairs were steep. And I heard her soft breathing, trying not to breathe.

She could hear me breathe.

Her soft throat, trying not to swallow. *(The amplified sound of The Voice gulping.)*

She could taste my saliva.

Her heart, trying not to beat. *(The amplified sound of a beating heart.)*

She could hear my heart thunder. *(The heart beats faster.)*

She knew I was there.

And I said: *"I'm Coming, Myrna."*

"I'm Coming . . . to Find . . . You . . ."

(Teresa Brewer's "Sweet Old Fashioned Girl" plays into the next scene.)

THE MONOGAMIST
by Christopher Kyle

(American) New York: Female

THE PLAY: After years of work, Dennis finally produces a volume of poetry suitable for publishing which earns him some acclaim. The theme? Monogamy. Inspired by his own writing, he finally marries his longtime lover, a professor of feminist literature. Soon, she is taken under the spell of one of her more charming male students, and she finds herself cheating on Dennis . . . what's more *Dennis* finds her cheating on Dennis. This leads Dennis to reciprocate with an equally young partner, and he finds Sky. As Dennis is forced to face the success of his book, the failure of his marriage, and the mentoring he must do with his new young lover, he begins to acknowledge the holes in his once strongly held, 60s-era philosophies.

THE MONOLOGUE: Sky (18 to 20) is getting stoned with Dennis and begins to describe her fascination with the sixties, an era Dennis can remember. The difference between the eighties and the sixties strikes her as pathetic, and she explains her reasons.

TIME AND PLACE: September 1991. Dennis's studio. Daytime.

NOTE: Avoid playing stoned. Just let the text speak for you.

SKY: *(She pours herself more Pernod.)* So what I'm saying is . . . What was I saying? Oh, yeah. About the sixties. The sixties were obviously this totally cool decade, you know, where everybody was whacked on some major drugs. And you had Morrison, Hendrix, Janis Joplin — all those fucking heroes — Mick Jagger. Okay? And Vietnam, which wasn't cool really, I guess, but it was definitely something to *care* about, and that's something about which I don't know *shit*. Caring, I mean. I want to get whacked, sure, but there's no . . . political content to it, okay? It's just people getting, you know, totally fucked up and wearing tie-dye shirts. It's a total rip-off of your whole culture and everybody knows it. Okay? Everybody knows it, which is, I guess, why it's cool. It's like totally fake and that's what's . . . *right* about it. It's like, hey — we don't give a shit about anything, but we're hip to it. Nobody's gonna blow us any shit. Nobody's gonna pull anything on us . . . like that Watergate, am I right? I bet that caught you by surprise. Not me. I knew what was going down and I was only *four years old.* It's like politics, you know? It's bogus. This whole country's all just . . . bogus. And that's why I voted for George Bush.

(Pause.)

I mean, the only thing that really *matters,* the only *issue,* is abortion. Okay? I mean, I could march on Washington or some bullshit for that. A woman should be able to choose. Choices — okay? — that's what it's all about. Options. Think about how few choices there used to be at McDonald's. When I was a kid there was, like, hamburger, cheeseburger, fries, shake. That's it. Now it takes half an hour to read the fucking menu. That's options. That's progress.

THE REINCARNATION OF JAIMIE BROWN
by Lynne Alvarez

American (New York): Female

THE PLAY: Set in and around New York City, Lynne Alvarez's play follows the life of Jaimie Brown, a street poet and the possible reincarnation of a wealthy tycoon's son. Street performer friends, wealthy lovers, mystical "reincarnation experts," and a complicated and involved case of mistaken identity are all woven together in this contemporary love adventure.

THE MONOLOGUE: At the top of the play, Jaimie (19) is "selling her wares" on the streets of New York.

TIME AND PLACE: New York City. The present. A busy street.

JAIMIE: Construction in New York's a bitch. *(She passes a doughnut stand, hands the vendor a sheet of paper, and grabs a doughnut. He starts to protest.)* Don't sweat it, man   in a couple years that'll be worth a fortune. I sign all my copies. A small investment now could set you up for life, you know what I mean? *(People pass, she tries to sell them a poem.)* You want a poem, Miss . . . uh you there, Miss, how about a poem? Thanks a lot. And you sir . . . a poem, an adventure — *(The man stops and looks her up and down lasciviously. Opens his raincoat and flashes Jaimie. Jaimie confronts him. As she walks forward, he walks back until at some point he turns and flees.)* not that kind of adventure, man, but thanks for sharing.

   I bet you and I are thinking alot of the same things right now. I'm out here selling poetry, but you're walking around naked under that raincoat with the same question burning between your . . . ah . . . ears.
   "What's happened to poetry in America?"
   Am I right?
   I mean when was the last time a poem
   rattled your bones?
   Well here I am to remedy that.
   Cast off, blast off.
   I'm the new wave poetry slave

I know what you're thinking — you have to study Elizabethan English to read poetry; you have to buy an arcane insane esoteric totally prosaic literary magazine available in only one bookstore on 47th street twice a year — am I correct?

Or you feel to hear a good poem you have to kneel at the knees of some MMP — Major Male Poet preferably facing his crotch.

Now tell me if that isn't true? Sad isn't it?

Well I say, no way

I give you your poetry straight

no rap, no rock, bee bop or hip hop

So how about five dollars, man?

You can afford it. Think of what you must save on clothes.

(The Flasher turns and runs.)

Yes, yes, yes

I'm the new wave poetry slave

the last living purist in America —

(David walks by with an instrument case. She looks him over.)

Well maybe I'm not all that pure,

Hey you — superdude.

Yeah you. What's up? *(She follows him.)*

You want a poem? A touch of culture, a touch of class

Love 'em and leave 'em right?

I have something just for you . . .

A road poem, a heartbreak poem, lonesome sexy blues.

BILOXI BLUES
by Neil Simon

American (New York): Male

THE PLAY: One of Simon's most popular, *Biloxi Blues* follows the hero, Eugene Jerome, through his army Basic Training at Fort Biloxi, Mississippi. He plans to "become a writer, not get killed and lose [his] virginity" during World War II. As he advances on his goals, he records the trials and tribulations of his training and the relationships of his corecruits in his journal. Through his narrative monologues, we are given insight into his burgeoning writer's perspective as the real-time scenes play out before our eyes.

THE MONOLOGUE: Arnold Epstein (18 to 22) is from New York and is very out-of-place in the Army. He recounts his evening for Jerome.

TIME AND PLACE: 1943. Fort Biloxi, Mississippi. Late evening. The barracks for new recruits.

ARNOLD: . . . I was in the latrine alone. I spent four hours cleaning it, on my hands and knees. It looked better than my mother's bathroom at home. Then these two non-coms come in, one was the cook, that three hundred pound guy and some other slob, with cigar butts in their mouths and reeking of beer . . . They come in to pee only instead of using the urinal, they use one of the johns, both peeing in the same one, making circles, figure-eights. Then they start to walk out and I say, "Hey, I just cleaned that. Please flush the johns." And the big one, the cook, says to me, "Up your ass, rookie," or some other really clever remark . . . And I block the doorway and I say, "There's a printed order on the wall signed by Captain Landon stating the regulations that all facilities must be flushed after using" . . . And I'm requesting that they follow regulations, since I was left in charge, and to please flush the facility . . . And the big one says to me, "Suppose you flush it, New York Jew Kike," and I said my ethnic heritage notwithstanding, please flush the facility . . . They look at each other, this half a ton of brainless beef and suddenly rush me, turn me upside down, grab my ankles and — and — and they lowered me by my feet with my head in the toilet, in their filth, their poison . . .

all the way until I couldn't breathe . . . then they pulled off my belt and tied my feet onto the ceiling pipes with my head still in their foul waste and tied my hands behind my back with dirty rags, and they left me there, hanging like a pig that was going to be slaughtered . . . I wasn't strong enough to fight back. I couldn't do it alone. No one came to help me . . . Then the pipe broke and I fell to the ground . . . It took me twenty minutes to get myself untied . . . Twenty minutes! . . . But it will take me the rest of my life to wash off my humiliation. I was degraded. I lost my dignity. If I stay, Gene, if they put a gun in my hands, one night, I swear to God, I'll kill them both . . . I'm not a murderer.

BILOXI BLUES
by Neil Simon

New York: Male

THE PLAY: One of Simon's most popular, *Biloxi Blues* follows the hero, Eugene Jerome, through his army Basic Training at Fort Biloxi, Mississippi. He plans to "become a writer, not get killed and lose [his] virginity" during World War II. As he advances on his goals, he records the trials and tribulations of his training and the relationships of his corecruits in his journal. Through his narrative monologues, we are given insight into his burgeoning writer's perspective as the real-time scenes play out before our eyes.

THE MONOLOGUE: Eugene Jerome's bunkmates have stolen his journal where he records his every impression and experience. They take turns reading what he's written about each of them. Arnold Epstein (18 to 22) takes the journal and begins to read it aloud, revealing for the first time his friend's true impression of him.

TIME AND PLACE: 1943. Fort Biloxi, Mississippi. Afternoon. The barracks for new recruits.

ARNOLD: Sure, Kowski. This is what we're fighting the war about, isn't it? *(He reads.)* "Arnold Epstein is truly the most complex and fascinating man I've ever met and his constant and relentless pursuit of truth, logic, and reason fascinates me in the same proportion as his obstinacy and unnecessary heroics drive me to distraction. But I love him for it. In the same manner that I love Joe DiMaggio for making the gesture of catching a long fly ball to center seem like the last miracle performed by God in modern times. But often I hold back showing my love and affection for Arnold because I think he might misinterpret it. It just happens to be my instinctive feeling — that Arnold is homosexual, and it bothers me that it bothers me." *(He closes the book. He looks at the others who are all staring at him.)* . . . Do you see why I find life so interesting? Here is a man of my own faith and background, potentially intelligent and talented, who in six weeks has come to the brilliant conclusion that a cretin like Wykowski is going to win the Medal of Honor and that I, his most esteemed and dearest friend, is a fairy. *(He tosses the book on Eugene's bunk.)* This is a problem worthy of a Talmudic scholar. Goodnight, fellas . . . It is my opinion that no one gets a wink of sleep tonight.

BILOXI BLUES
by Neil Simon

American (New York): Male

THE PLAY: One of Simon's most popular, *Biloxi Blues* follows the hero, Eugene Jerome, through his army Basic Training at Fort Biloxi, Mississippi. He plans to "become a writer, not get killed and lose [his] virginity" during World War II. As he advances on his goals, he records the trials and tribulations of his training and the relationships of his corecruits in his journal. Through his narrative monologues, we are given insight into his burgeoning writer's perspective as the real-time scenes play out before our eyes.

THE MONOLOGUE: Eugene Jerome (18 to 22) has achieved one of his goals — he has lost his virginity to a woman his buddies paid (Rowena). The experience was not all that he thought it would be, and now he yearns to find a true love. In his stylistic addresses to the audience, we hear his "journal" thoughts.

TIME AND PLACE: 1943. "Limbo." (The characters are in Basic Training at Fort Biloxi, Mississippi)

Light up on Eugene in limbo.

EUGENE: *(To audience.)* . . . I felt real lousy about Hennesey . . . The next weekend I went to Rowena's again . . . She didn't even remember me . . . She acted like I was a stranger . . . I tell her about Hennesey doing it with another guy and maybe getting five years in jail and she says, "Well, I haven't got too much sympathy for their kind, sweetheart. They're just taking the bread out of the mouths of my babies" . . . I'm never going to pay for it again . . . It just cheapens the whole idea of sex . . . *(The sets begin to change into the U.S.O.)* . . . I was determined to meet the perfect girl. I knew just what she would be like . . . She's going to be pretty but not too beautiful. When they're too beautiful, they love them first and you second . . . And she'll be athletic. Someone I could hit fly balls to and she'd catch all of them. She'll love to go to the movies and read books and see plays and we'd never run out of conversation . . . She's out there, I know it. Right now the girl I'm going to fall in love with is living in New York or Boston or Philadelphia — walking around the streets, not even knowing I'm alive. It's crazy. *(Light up on U.S.O. Daisy dancing with a soldier.)* — There she is and here I am. The both of us just waiting around to meet. Why doesn't she just yell out, "Eugene! I'm here! Come and get me" . . . *(The dance ends. Soldier goes off. Daisy crosses to Eugene.)*

BOYS' LIFE
by Howard Korder

American (New York): Male

THE PLAY: Through a series of vignettes, the angst of relationships and the passing of time is revealed in the lives of urbanites in their late 20s.

THE MONOLOGUE: Phil (25 to 29) bumps into his ex-girlfriend at a party. The moment is awkward. Phil attempts to strike up a conversation with the woman he hasn't quite gotten over yet.

TIME AND PLACE: The present. Later evening. A child's bedroom where the coats of the party guests have been piled on top of the bed. A big city.

PHIL: [Hmmm? Oh, sure.] Things are going really really great for me right now. Just fine. I have my own partition now, over at the office, they put up one of those, ah . . . so *that's* really good. And I'm going to the spa a lot, I'm working ou — well, I can't use the machines 'cause you know of my back, but I love the Jacuzzi, so, actually, it's strange, 'cause I fell asleep in it, in the whirlpool, and when I woke up I had this incredible headache. I mean it would *not* go away. I felt this thing here like the size of a peach pit, I went for a *blood* test, I was convinced I, you hear all this stuff now, the way it's spreading. I mean I'm not — but I was sure I had it.
It. You know.
(Pause.)
I didn't. So.
(Pause. Karen looks at the door.)
Anyway, it's funny we both happened to turn up here tonight, isn't it, 'cause I was just thinking, I was wondering . . . I mean, it's a couple of months since I last spoke to you and I was just *wondering* if we were still, you know, seeing each other.

BOYS' LIFE
by Howard Korder

American (New York): Male

THE PLAY: Through a series of vignettes, the angst of relationships and the passing of time is revealed in the lives of urbanites in their late 20s.

THE MONOLOGUE: Phil (25 to 29) has had a series of failed relationships. He is nearing the lowest point of his life. As he and his buddy Jack watch Jack's son play at the park, Phil reveals the torment his latest relationship has caused him. Jack is less than compassionate to him.

TIME AND PLACE: A city park. A bench. The present.

The park. Jack and Phil sitting on a bench. Jack with a child's toy in his hand. Phil looking out front.

PHIL: I would have destroyed myself for this woman. Gladly. I would have eaten garbage. I would have sliced my *wrists* open. Under the right circumstances, I mean, if she said, "Hey, Phil, why don't you just cut your wrists open," well, come on, but if *seriously* . . . We clicked, we connected on so many things, right off the bat, we talked about God for *three hours* once, I don't know what good it did, but that *intensity* . . . and the first time we went to bed, I didn't even touch her. I didn't *want* to, understand what I'm saying? And you know, I played it very casually, because, all right, I've had some rough experiences, I'm the first to admit, but after a couple of weeks I could feel we were right there, so I laid it down, everything I wanted to tell her, and . . . and she says to me . . . she says . . . "Nobody should ever need another person that badly." Do you *believe* that? "Nobody should ever . . ."! What is that? Is that something you saw on TV? I dump my *heart* on the table, you give me Joyce Dr. Fucking Brothers? "Need, need," I'm saying I *love* you, is that wrong? Is that not allowed anymore?
    (Pause. Jack looks at him.)
    And so what if I did need her? Is that so bad? All right, crucify me, I needed her! So *what!* I don't want to be by myself, I'm by myself I feel like I'm going out of my mind, I do. I sit there, I'm thinking forget it,

I'm not gonna make it through the next *ten seconds,* I just can't *stand* it. But I do, somehow, I get through the ten seconds, but then I have to do it all over again, 'cause they just keep coming, all these . . . seconds, floating by, while I'm waiting for something to happen, I don't know what, a car wreck, a nuclear war or something, that sounds awful but at least there'd be this *instant* when I'd know I was alive. Just once. 'Cause I look in the mirror, and I can't believe I'm really there. I can't believe that's me. It's like my body, right, is the size of, what, the Statue of Liberty, and I'm inside it, I'm down in one of the legs, this gigantic hairy leg. I'm scraping around inside my own foot like some tiny fetus. And I don't know who I am, or where I'm going. And I wish I'd never been born. *(Pause.)* Plus, my hair is falling out, that really *sucks.*

BRIGHTON BEACH MEMOIRS
by Neil Simon

American (New York): Male

THE PLAY: The first of Simon's famous and popular memoir trilogy (followed by *Biloxi Blues* and *Broadway Bound*), in *Brighton Beach Memoirs* we are introduced to the rich and fascinating characters in the life of aspiring writer, Eugene Jerome. The extended Jerome family is large and crowded into a single-family wooden frame house in Brighton Beach. Eugene Jerome records not only his puberty and burgeoning interest in things beyond baseball but also observes and records the dramas (large and small) that occur in the lives of his mother, aunt, father, brother, and cousins as they live out one week in September 1937.

THE MONOLOGUE: Eugene Jerome (almost 15) is beginning his writing career by keeping a diary of his thoughts, observations, and desires. Very complete in his entries, he records his family history and relationships as well. As he writes, he talks to the audience.

TIME AND PLACE: Eugene's half of the bedroom. His house. Brighton Beach, Brooklyn, New York. 6:30 PM. September 1937.

EUGENE: *(Writing, says aloud.)* "That's-what-they-have-gutters-for" . . . *(To audience.)* If my mother knew I was writing all this down, she would stuff me like one of her chickens . . . I'd better explain what she meant by Aunt Blanche's "situation" . . . You see, her husband, Uncle Dave, died six years ago from . . . *(He looks around.)* . . . this thing . . . They never say the word. They always whisper it. It was — *(He whispers.)* — Cancer! . . . I think they're afraid if they said it out loud, God would say, "I HEARD THAT! YOU SAID THE DREAD DISEASE! *(He points finger down.)* JUST FOR THAT, I SMITE YOU DOWN WITH IT!!" . . . There are some things that grown-ups just won't discuss . . . For example, my grandfather. He died from — *(He whispers.)* — Diptheria! . . . Anyway, after Uncle Dave died, he left Aunt Blanche with no money. Not even insurance . . . And she couldn't support herself because she has — *(She whispers.)* — Asthma . . . So my big-hearted mother insisted we take her and her kids in to live with us. So they broke up our room into two small rooms and me and my brother Stan live on this side, and Laurie and her sister Nora live on the other side. My father thought it would just be temporary, but it's been three and a half years so far and I think because of Aunt Blanche's situation, my father is developing — *(He whispers.)* — High blood pressure!

DEAD END
by Sidney Kingsley

American (New York): Male

THE PLAY: A classic, gritty American realism play, *Dead End* paints the portrait of a New York neighborhood in the midst of gentrification. The poor, dirty neighborhood regulars find themselves with new neighbors — the wealthy residents of a private new apartment complex (The East River Terrace Apartments). As the boys of the neighborhood swim in the murky, polluted East River, their wealthy neighbors are treated to an indoor pool and all the best amenities. The friction between the haves and the have-nots builds throughout the play, erupting in a final tragic ending.

THE MONOLOGUE: Martin (28) is a local legend. Known to the rest of the world as Baby-Face Martin, he returned to his old neighborhood to look up his mother and the girl he never forgot. He runs into his childhood pal, Gimpty, and is immediately worried that Gimpty might turn him in for the reward money. Gimpty assures Martin that he would never do that and wonders to Martin why he chose the life he chose.

TIME AND PLACE: 1935. A dead end of a New York street, ending in a wharf over the East River, near the East Fifties. Late afternoon.

MARTIN: Den don' gimme any a dat crap! What ta hell did yuh tink I wuz gonna do, hang aroun' 'is dump waitin' fer Santa Claus tuh take care a me, fer Chris' sake? Looka yew! What a yew got? Six years yuh went tuh college an what da hell a yuh got? A lousy handout a thoity bucks a month! Not fer me! I yain't like yew punks . . . starvin' an' freezin' . . . fuh what? Peanuts? Coffee an'? Yeah, I got mine, but I took it. Look! *(Pulls at his shirt.)* Silk. Twenty bucks. Look a dis! *(Pulls at his jacket.)* Custom tailored — a hunderd an' fifty bucks. Da fat a da land I live off of. An' I got a flock a dames at'd make yew guys water at da mout'. At'd make yew slobs run off in a dark corner when yuh see dere pichure an play pocket-pool.

What ta hell, yuh can't live faever. Ah, I don' know. Sure! Sometimes I git da jitters. An' sometimes I git a terrific yen' tuh stay put, an' . . . Ah, ta hell wid it! Say, do yew remember dat kid Francey?

She wuz my goil when we were kids.

Ey don' make no more like her. I know. I had 'em all. Yuh ain't seen her around, have yuh?

Hoid anythin' about her?

Gee, I got a terrific yen tuh see dat kid again. At's why I come back here. I wonder what she's doin'. Maybe she got married. Nah, she couldn'! Maybe she died. Nah, not Francey! She had too much on a ball, too much stuff . . . guts. Yeah, she wuz like me. Nuttin' kin kill Baby-Face Martin an' nuttin' kin kill her. Not Francey. Gese, I wonder what's become a her?

DEAD END
by Sidney Kingsley

New York: Male

THE PLAY: A classic, gritty American realism play, *Dead End* paints the portrait of a New York neighborhood in the midst of gentrification. The poor, dirty neighborhood regulars find themselves with new neighbors — the wealthy residents of a private new apartment complex (The East River Terrace Apartments). As the boys of the neighborhood swim in the murky, polluted East River, their wealthy neighbors are treated to an indoor pool and all the best amenities. The friction between the haves and the have-nots builds throughout the play, erupting in a final tragic ending.

THE MONOLOGUE: Gimpty (22 to 24) has been crippled in the leg by rickets since he was a child. He was able to get out of the neighborhood for a little while and send himself to school. Trained as an architect, he hasn't been working lately, and his poverty is beginning to get to him . . . especially since he's fallen in love with one of the wealthy residents of the Terrace Apartments. His inability to give her the life she deserves weighs on his soul as he prepares to see her off on her sailing trip.

TIME AND PLACE: 1935. A dead end of a New York street, ending in a wharf over the East River, near the East Fifties. Night.

GIMPTY: *(Stares down at the black water swirling under him. He begins to talk, faster and faster, trying to push back into his unconscious the terror that haunts him, to forget that afternoon if only for a few seconds.)* It reminds me of something . . . What is it? . . . Oh, yeah . . . when I was a kid. In the spring the sudden sun showers used to flood the gutters. The other kids used to race boats down the street. Little boats: straws, matches, lollipopsticks. I couldn't run after them, so I guarded the sewer and caught the boats to keep them from tumbling in. Near the sewer . . . sometimes, I remember . . . a whirlpool would form . . . Dirt and oil from the street would break into rainbow colors . . . iridescent . . . *(For a moment he does escape.)* Beautiful, I think . . . a marvel of color out of dirty water. I can't take my eyes off it. And suddenly a boat in danger. *(The terror in him rises again.)* I try to stop it . . . Too late! It shoots into the black hole of the sewer. I used to dream about falling into it myself. The river reminds me of that . . . Death must be like this . . . like the river at night. *(There is no comfort in her big enough for his needs. They sit in brooding silence, which is finally interrupted by the Doorman's voice, off.)*

A HATFUL OF RAIN
by Michael Gazzo

American (New York): Male

THE PLAY: A dramatic look at the life of a young man and the effects of drug addiction. Set in a New York tenement apartment, the story follows the troubles of Johnny, a young Army vet who was wounded during his tour of service and became addicted to the drugs he was given in the hospital. As he tries to take care of his wife and the baby on the way, he tries just as desperately to keep his addiction a secret.

THE MONOLOGUE: Johnny (20 to 22) has been out all night again and is finding it more and more difficult to come up with an adequate excuse for absence. Asked by his wife, once again, where he was the night before, Johnny tries to convince her of his good intentions.

TIME AND PLACE: 1950s. An apartment living room/kitchen area in New York's Lower East Side. Early evening.

JOHNNY: *(Crosses to her.)* This morning you said that the marriage was a bust, that we were on the rocks — After you left — Did you ever feel like you were going crazy? Ever since I knew the old man was coming up — I just can't stop remembering things — like all night long I've been hearing that whistle — The old man used to whistle like that when he used to call us — I was supposed to come right home from school, but I played marbles. Maybe every half hour he'd whistle — I'd be on my knees in the schoolyard, with my immie glove on — you take a woman's gloves and you cut off the fingers — so your fingers are free and your knuckles don't bleed in the wintertime — and I just kept on playing and the whistle got madder and madder. It starts to get dark and I'd get worried but I wouldn't go home until I won all the marbles — and he'd be up on that porch whistling away. I'd cross myself at the door — there was a grandmother I had who taught me to cross myself to protect myself from lightning — I'd open the door and go in — hold up the chamois bag of marbles and I'd say, hey, Pop, I won! Wham! Pow! — I'd wind up in the corner saying Pop, I didn't hear you. I didn't hear you —

(Johnny sits in chair.)
I'm trying to tell you what I did today —

I took a train see — then I took a bus — I went to look at the house I was born in. It's only an hour away — but in fifteen years, I've never gone anywhere near that house — or that town! I had to go back — I can't explain the feeling, but I was ten years old when I left there — The way I looked around, they must have thought I was crazy — because I kept staring at the old house — I was going to knock at the door and ask the people if I could just look around — and then I went to that Saybrook school where I used to hear the old man whistle — and those orange fire-escapes — and ivy still climbing up the walls. *(Rises — crosses to Center.)* Then I took the bus and the train, and I went to meet the old man's plane — and we came here.

THE INDIAN WANTS THE BRONX
by Israel Horowitz

American (New York): Male

THE PLAY: Horowitz's stark presentation of two tough New York hoodlums
challenges today's politically correct and sensitive audiences with its
overt harshness and cruelty. However, beyond the surface of violence
that the young men exhibit lie the souls of lost youth who have run out
of hope.

THE MONOLOGUE: Joey (20 to 22) has become the more friendly of the two
bullies, and as Murph leaves and lets off some steam, Joey opens up to
an old man from India about the depth of his friend's pain and anger.

TIME AND PLACE: A bus stop on upper Fifth Avenue, New York City. A chilly
evening. September. The present.

JOEY: Murph's my best buddy, you know. Me and him were buddies when we
were kids. Me and Murph, all the time. And Maggie. His kid sister.
(Pause.) I had Maggie once. Sort of. Well, kind of. Yeah, I had her. That's
right. Murph don't know. Makes no difference now. She's dead, Maggie.
Makes no difference when you're dead. *(Sings.)* The worms crawl in. The
worms crawl out. *(Speaks.)* What the hell difference does it make? Right?
(Without noticing.) That's why Murph is crazy. That's why he gets crazy,
I mean. She dies seventeen, that's all. Seventeen. Just like *that*. Appendix.
No one around. There was no one around. His old lady? Forget it! The
old man took off years ago. All there was really was just Murph and
Maggie. That's why he could take it. At home. You think my old lady's
bad. She's nothing. His old lady's a pro. You know? She don't even make
a living at it, either. That's the bitch of it. Not even a living. She's a dog.
I mean, *I* wouldn't even pay her a nickel. Not a nickel. Not that I'd screw
around with Murph's old lady. Oh! Not that she doesn't try. She tries.
Plenty. *(His fantasy begins.)* That's why I don't come around to his house
much. She tries all the time. She wouldn't charge me anything, probably. But it ain't right screwing your best buddy's old lady, right? I'd feel
terrible if I did. She ain't that bad, but it just ain't right. I'd bet she'd even
take Murph on. She probably tries it with him, too. That's the bitch of

it. She can't even make a living. You think Pussyface is a help? That's the biggest joke yet. *(The Indian is by now thoroughly confused on all counts. He recognizes the name Pussyface and reacts slightly. Seeing Joey's anxiety, he cuddles him. For a brief moment, they embrace: an insane father-and-son tableau. Note: Be careful here. I. H.)* Pussyface. There's a brain. You see what she gave us for Christmas. *(He fishes a knife out of his pocket.)* Knives. Brilliant, huh? Murph's up on a rap for slicing a kid and she gives us knives for Christmas. To whittle with. She's crazier than Murphy.

SECTION FIVE

AMERICAN

(Southern)

AMERICAN (SOUTHERN)
INTRODUCTION

Most Americans find it relatively simple to imitate a Southern accent. We are exposed to it in many different arenas — films, television shows, and the evening news. The South is a place of history, mystery, and ideals and is compelling in its stories and personalities.

American actors, at some point in their careers, will have to do a Southern accent. It is practically unavoidable. So many great plays have been written both *about* the South and *by* Southern authors that one would have to make a conscious effort to avoid them to never do a Southern accent!

Traditionally, when one first attempts a Southern accent, it is with a sense of the ridiculous. We put on a Southern accent when we want to sound dumb or when we imitate an intense preacher. These two insulting stereotypes have pervaded the American consciousness so deeply, that it becomes a challenge to change our way of thinking about the Southern accent. Indeed, as a Dialect Coach, I have found that my Southern friends who serve as primary sources for the sound changes I use, are very suspicious of anyone else attempting to do a Southern accent. They feel that it will always come out sounding stereotypical, "hick," and not true.

To resist the urge to do a stereotypical accent, it is up to the actor to research the history and sociology of his or her character thoroughly. The actor must know what his or her character's educational level is, what his or her influences were growing up, where he or she is from, and what that means to the language of the people around that character.

The Southern accents vary greatly depending on where you are in the South. Places east of the Mississippi River tend to have a bit more drawl and slightly softer *r*'s than places west of the Mississippi. The original settlers of the land have an influence on the evolution of the dialect; for example, when the Welsh settlers arrived in western North Carolina, they kept moving farther and farther inland toward the mountains that reminded them of home. The very specific Appalachian Mountain dialect can possibly be traced back to those original Welsh settlers and their unique Welsh dialect! Likewise, the original British inhabitants of Georgia may have had a lasting impact on the very proper, British-sounding, Georgia dialect.

For the most part, a general, well-done Texas dialect will serve you as the most common Southern dialect used in scene study classes or on stage. As with each dialect you study, you must read the entire play and character descriptions to accurately place your accent. What follow are some general sound substitutions that should give you a wide representation of the sounds of the South.

- The Southern drawl is achieved by saying a slight *uh* sound before or after you say a pure vowel sound (like the sound *ay* may become *uhay*). It is not separate from the pure vowel, but is done almost at the same time as the vowel, very quickly and subtly. The vowel sound moves around a bit.
- Depending on where you are, the pace of the Southern dialect can vary from the extremes of incredibly quick and piercing to slow and syrupy. Different paces of speech lie between those two extremes.
- Southern dialects are spoken with the lips and tongue relaxed. This will give you a feeling of total throat and facial relaxation. This does not suggest a lack of energy, but rather an ease in the speech and rhythm of the dialect/character. This dialect can feel relaxing and comfortable.
- If you overdo the drawl or the relaxation element of the dialect, your character will seem stereotypical and caricatured. Be careful.
- Subtlety works well in this dialect. You may not need to change much in your own speech pattern to achieve this dialect. In fact, adopting only a few of the suggested changes may give you enough of a southern sound to lend your character some credibility.
- Warm up your facial muscles and do some jaw-releasing exercises before working on this dialect; the more free and relaxed your face is, the more relaxed and free your sounds will become.

Southern Film, Television, and Audio References

Film

Texas:
The Apostle
A Time to Kill
Contact
Places in the Heart
Raising Arizona
Broadcast News
Perfect Harmony
Trip to Bountiful
1918
Courtship
Come Back to the Five and Dime,
   Jimmy Dean, Jimmy Dean

Alabama/Mississippi:
Double Jeopardy
Forrest Gump
Steel Magnolias
Ghosts of Mississippi
Mississippi Burning
Cat on a Hot Tin Roof
Fried Green Tomatoes
To Kill a Mockingbird

Georgia/Deep South/Plantation:
The Gift
Midnight in the Garden of Good and Evil
Beloved
Passion Fish
Deliverance
The Color Purple
Gone With the Wind
Driving Miss Daisy

Tennessee/Arkansas:
Sling Blade
Nine to Five
Best Little Whorehouse in Texas
Rhinestone
The River Rat

Television
"Beverly Hillbillies"
"Designing Women"
"Empty Nest"

"Golden Girls"
"Grace Under Fire"
"In the Heat of the Night"

DIALECT TAPES AND SOURCES

American Southern Dialects	Gillian Lane-Plescia
American Southern Dialects (2)	Gillian Lane-Plescia
Stage Dialects	Jerry Blunt
More Stage Dialects	Jerry Blunt
Dialects for the Stage	Evangeline Machlin
Acting with an Accent — American South	David Alan Stern
IDEA website	www.ukans.edu/~idea/index.html

For a more complete and detailed list of films/resources, see Ginny Kopf's book The Dialect Handbook.

SOUTHERN SOUNDS

Southern vowel changes:

ih	→ eeuh	this, his	→ theeyus, heeyuz
a	→ a or ayuh	man, can	→ mayuhn, cayuhn
ow	→ a	how, now	→ ha,na
oh	→ uhoh	goes, show	→ guhohz, shuhoh
aw	→ ah	all, tall	→ ahl, tahl
uh	→ uh (relaxed)	of, dove	→ uhv, duhv
eh	→ ih	ten, men	→ tin, min
eye	→ ah	night, right	→ naht, raht
ay	→ uhay	paper, day	→ puhaypuh, duhay
oo	→ uhoo	routes, news	→ ruhoots, nuhooz

The *r* dipthongs:

ear	→ eer or eeuh	here, dear	→ heeyuh, deeyuh
or	→ ohr or owuh	your, more	→ yowuh, mowuh
air	→ ehyuh or air	there, where	→ theyuh, whehyuh
are	→ ah or are	cart, large	→ caht, lahge

Southern consonant changes:

[r]		dropped in some regions, hardened in others
[ing]	→ [in]	bikin', hikin', farmin'

Some special word pronunciations in the South:

Sir = suh
can't = kaint
-day (of the week) = dih

Southern Practice Sentences

[ih] → [eeuh]:
  This is his distant cousin Isabelle. His fist hit the tip of his brim.

[a] → [a or ayuh]:
  The man's plan was hard to understand. Can Stan give the land to Nan?

[ow] → [a]:
  How do the cows know how to plow? Around town, I wear a crown.

[oh] → [uhoh]:
  Oh, Joe, you know how it goes. Don't go to the road show . . . it's slow.

[aw] → [ah]:
  All the lawyers are tall and may fall. Crawl through the hall.

[uh] → [uh (relaxed)]:
  The Doves of Love are from Lubbock. With my gloves, I scrubbed my tub clean.

[eh] → [ih]:
  Ten of the seventeen men were from Tennessee. Get the pen from the pen center.

[eye] → [ah]:
  The night was white with the light from the sky. Moonlight is right for flight.

[ay] → [uhay]:
  Take the paper from the Mayor to the Lady of the Lake. The day is going away.

[oo] → [uhoo]:
  The two of you are blue in the tooth. I grew two foot in two weeks!

[or] → [ohr or ohuh]:
  Your four-year-old broke the store horsey. Go ye forth and multiply!

[ear] → [eer or eeuh]:
  Here is your beer, Dear. The deer is afeared of the rearview mirror.

A BIRD OF PREY
by Jim Grimsley

American (Southern): Female

THE PLAY: Set in an urban environment, *A Bird of Prey* takes a harsh, grim view of the dangers that plague and tempt the lives of today's teens. Centered around the story of Monty and his family's turbulent move from Louisiana, the cruelties of peer pressure are given a stark twist in this drama.

THE MONOLOGUE: Marie (15) is new to town and has just begun to make friends. As she waits for her older brothers to come and pick her up, she reveals her true feelings about her home life and the life she wishes she had.

TIME AND PLACE: Afternoon. Outside of a school in an urban environment. The present day.

The Angels sit close together, waiting, as Marie enters to one of the upper levels and faces the audience.

MARIE: I'm going home, I'm walking behind Monty and Evan, and I'm being quiet so Evan won't punch me in the shoulder, I'm going home like I'm supposed to, but I don't want to go. All day in school it's been peaceful, with nobody bothering me, except Marie in my math class who hates that we have the same name. Except for her they leave me alone, and I like that. All day I sit there with my books and do what I'm supposed to do. Everything is calm all day. But school doesn't last long enough, I have to go home at the end of every day, and when the bell rings I get all hollow inside, and I pack up my books and go outside to wait for Monty and Evan. We walk home the long way, we go pretty slow, and we never talk, unless we're arguing about something. We're all thinking the same thing, we're all wondering what it will be like when we get home, and I hate that feeling, I hate not knowing. I wish it would be peaceful, I think about it the whole way home, and sometimes it is. Sometimes Mama comes to walk us home instead of Monty, and I can tell by the way she looks whether it's okay at home or not. If she's smiling and she's brushed her hair and if she looks me in the eye, then every-thing's all right. But if she's standing there with her arms all wrapped around herself and her hair pulled back and she's looking at the ground, I know it's not okay, I know they're fighting again. I don't want to go home then, more than anything. But I don't have any choice. I wish school lasted longer. Sometimes I wish it lasted so long I would have to spend the night. I told that to my friend Candy, we have most of our classes together, and she likes me; I told her I wish I could stay in school all the time, but she didn't understand. She says I need a boyfriend, that's all I need, but I think about my dad and I don't know if I want one or not. *(Marie lingers on stages as lights on her go down.)*

COME BACK TO THE FIVE AND DIME, JIMMY DEAN, JIMMY DEAN
by Ed Graczyk

American (Southern): Female

THE PLAY: Using flashbacks and real time, the story of the "Disciples of James Dean" is told. We see the young beginnings of the adults they become as old friends gather for a reunion at their childhood club.

THE MONOLOGUE: Mona (17), and her future counterpart, retells the story of her evening with James Dean. In this first part of the memory, she describes the frenzy created in Texas when the filming of *Giant* was happening.

TIME AND PLACE: Mid-September. 1955. A rural town in Texas, somewhere near Marfa, where the movie *Giant* was made. The local five and dime store.

MONA (THEN): Well, you all know how everyone in town was just buzzin' when it was announced over the radio they were lookin' for people to be in it.

 It was like a regular parade. People from all over these parts headed for Marfa, bumper to bumper, to be in that movie. Joe borrowed his . . . Joe borrowed his mama's Buick and . . .

 . . . right after work we drove off into the sunset, laughin' an' gigglin' an' pretendin' like it was the end of a movie. It hadn't even begun yet, that was the funny part. We were playin' the endin' an' the beginnin' was yet to come. I pretended I was Natalie Wood and Joe . . .

 There were nearly four thousand . . .

 . . . people in that small town when we got there. All the rooms in the Paisano Hotel were filled-up, so Joe an' I had to sleep in the Buick along the side of the road.

 Next mornin' . . .

 . . . after I had washed up in the sink of the gas station across the road, nearly rubbin' my skin off with Boraxo an' paper towels . . .

I was sittin' in the back seat of the Buick pourin' lilac perfume all over to get rid of the smell of the Boraxo, when I saw "him" walkin' down the road, right toward me.

. . . an' he stopped right next to the car, lookin' in his pocket for somethin'. There was a cigarette danglin' from out of the corner of his mouth. So I took a chance that a match was what he was huntin' for and I leaned out the car window an' says . . . "I've got a match, if that's what you're needin'." He sort of smiled an' took the matches just like he had been livin' in Texas all his life.

(Taking a lace handkerchief out of her dress pocket and unfolds it.) And here are the matches that he touched. *(Sissy (Then), Stella, and Edna squeal and lean over them.)* Careful now . . . you might wipe the fingerprints off.

When he lit his cigarette and I looked up into them deep-set, sky-blue eyes . . . I could see myself, clear as lookin' in a mirror. It was at that very moment I knew somethin' was gonna happen to change my whole life.

Later on at the place where they were pickin' people to be in the movie . . . an' they picked me . .. me, out of all them hundreds of others . . . I knew for certain!

COME BACK TO THE FIVE AND DIME, JIMMY DEAN, JIMMY DEAN
by Ed Graczyk

American (Southern): Female

THE PLAY: Using flashbacks and real time, the story of the "Disciples of James Dean" is told. We see the young beginnings of the adults they become as old friends gather for a reunion at their childhood club.

THE MONOLOGUE: Mona (17), and her future counterpart, retells the story of her evening with James Dean. In this second part of the memory, she recounts the magical evening she "spent" with James Dean after her day of filming.

TIME AND PLACE: Mid-September. 1955. A rural town in Texas, somewhere near Marfa, where the movie *Giant* was made. The local five & dime store.

MONA (THEN): I felt like such a celebrity the way they were all fussin' over me.
  That night I laid there in the back seat of the Buick and kept thinkin' about how I was chosen above all them thousands of others . . . starin' out the window at the millions of stars an' the outline of that beautiful house way off in the distance. Suddenly, one of those stars exploded, burst away from all the others an' fell from the sky . . . landin' right behin' the house . . . behin' the front of Reata. I leaned over the seat to point it out to Joe, but he had tramped off somewhere, all mad 'cause he wasn't chosen, too.
  I pulled my blanket aroun' my shoulders an' started to walk to where the star had fallen to earth. I walked past the front gate down the road to the house. It was so quiet and still . . . the only sound was comin' from a far away train, blowin' its whistle an' chuggin' off into the night. When I got to the front porch, this voice comin' outta nowhere says, "Isn't it a little late to be callin' on your neighbors?" It was him. I knew it. I knew it the first minute I heard his voice. Then he said, "Don't just stand there bein' unfriendly. Come on up on the porch an' sit a spell." As I moved up the stairs, I reminded him that I was the one who

gave him a match that mornin' . . . and he thanked me again. We spent that whole entire night together . . . until the sun started to peek out from over the edge of the earth, turnin' the sky into the brightest red I ever saw.

(Sharply to Joe.) We walked together to the gate an' he thanked me for sharin' the night with him an' then we both walked away in separate directions.

CURSE OF THE STARVING CLASS
by Sam Shepard

American (Southern): Female

THE PLAY: A surreal exploration of a twisted family and their relationships with each other, *Curse of the Starving Class* is a dark study of the lives of a poor, rural family. As the father drinks the farm away, and the mother schemes to sell it and move to Europe, the daughter tries to rise above her shallow roots as her brother begins his walk down the same path as his father.

THE MONOLOGUE: Emma (12 to 13) and Wesley are left to fend for themselves often as their parents scheme and betray each other. Emma is just as flighty as her mother, and she dreams of leaving her home someday and becoming a "miraculous" mechanic in Mexico. Here, she tells Wesley how she would exact her revenge on her mother and the lawyer who is trying to steal their farm.

TIME AND PLACE: A farm (not necessarily in the South). The kitchen. Morning.

EMMA: *(Pause, as they work.)* They're probably half way to Mexico by now.
[WESLEY: Who?]
EMMA: She snuggling up to him and giggling and turning the dial on the radio. He's feeling proud of himself. He's buying her hot dogs and bragging about his business.
[WESLEY: She'll be back.]
EMMA: She's telling him all about us and about how Dad's crazy and trying to kill her all the time. She's happy to be on the road. To see new places go flashing by. They cross the border and gamble on the jai alai games. They head for Baja and swim along the beaches. They build campfires and roast fish at night. In the morning they take off again. But they break down somewhere outside a little place called Los Cerritos. They have to hike five miles into town. They come to a small beat-up gas station with one pump and a dog with three legs. There's only one mechanic in the whole town, and that's me. They don't recognize me though. They ask if I can fix their "carro," and I speak only Spanish. I've

lost the knack for English by now. I understand them though and give them a lift back up the road in my rebuilt four-wheel-drive International. I jump out and look inside the hood. I see that it's only the rotor inside the distributor that's broken, but I tell them that it needs an entire new generator, a new coil, points and plugs, and some slight adjustments to the carburetor. It's an overnight job, and I'll have to charge them for labor. So I set a cot up for them in the garage, and after they've fallen asleep I take out the entire engine and put in a rebuilt Volkswagen block. In the morning I charge them double for labor, see them on their way, and then resell their engine for a small mint.

CYRA AND ROCKY
by Cherie Bennett

American (Southern): Female

THE PLAY: A contemporary version of the story of Cyrano de Bergerac, *Cyra and Rocky* is a reversed-role interpretation of the famous tale of deception and love. Forced to write to each other because of an English assignment, Chrissy and Rocky begin, begrudgingly, to exchange letters (she lives in Nashville, he lives in Michigan). When they reach high school, and the assignment continues and includes sending a photo of themselves along with the next letter, their interest in each other grows as each discovers how attractive the other is. That is when Chrissy enlists the help of Cyra, her best friend and a far more poetic and articulate writer. Rocky begins to fall in love with Chrissy's (actually Cyra's) letters and plans to meet Chrissy in person. In typical Cyrano fashion, there is deception, true friendship, and the discovery of the real heart behind the words that Rocky hears.

THE MONOLOGUE: Cyra (14) has just been insulted by Rocky's friend, Brett, but he can't stand up to her in a battle of wits.

TIME AND PLACE: Present. Near a park where people skateboard. Nashville, Tennessee.

CYRA: Well, he can. But he's just so . . . so dull. So uninspired. Such a major yawn. If you're going to insult me, or disrespect me — or *dis* me, as it were, you could at least be creative about it, Brett! Let me give you a few examples. From an investment point of view: "If I was as big as you are, I'd take out some major stock in Jenny Craig!" Being friendly: "Hey, Big Beauty, I bet you could do the wave all by yourself!" Pro sports fan: "The Jets are seriously desperate for an offensive line, and I think you're their woman!" The religious dis: "I fear that she's so fat even God Himself couldn't lift her spirits!" The Wizard of Oz dis: "Gosh, Toto, we're not in Kansas anymore; she IS Kansas!" The Southern dis: *(In a syrupy accent.)* "Why, honey, if we could have dropped you on the battle of Gettysburg, we would have won that wo-ah." The fashion dis: "I know those aren't 501 jeans you're wearing, they must be 747s!" The Hallmark card: "Your birthday is so special, I hope it will be pleasant, so sorry I'm empty-handed, but you sat upon your present." And finally, the Save-the-Whales dis: "Woah, I bet when you go to the beach little kids start yelling 'Free Willy! Free Willy!'"

Those are some of the things you *could* have said, Brett, if you were clever. And here's a few of the things I *could* have said to someone as dull witted as you, no offense, if I wasn't such a nice person: The first-grader dis: "When you asked your teacher what letter came after X, she said 'Y,' and you said, ''cause I wanna know.'" The raise-the-unemployment-rate dis: "I heard you got a job as an elevator operator, but they fired you when you couldn't memorize the route." The canceled-vacation dis: "When you drove to catch your flight and saw the sign that says 'airport left,' you turned around and went home." Brett, you're so slow you need a recipe for ice cubes, you could be a poster child for a rock pile, you'd bungee-jump off my shoelaces, and finally, in closing, if I asked you for a penny for your thoughts, I'd feel morally obligated to GIVE YOU CHANGE! *(Chrissy and Rocky cheer and applaud wildly. Brett is mortified.)*

THE DARKER FACE OF THE EARTH
by Rita Dove

American (Southern): Female

THE PLAY: In this retelling of the classic Greek tragedy, Rita Dove sets the *Oedipus* story on a South Carolina plantation in the antebellum (1820–1840) South. A white plantation owner's daughter has an affair with one of their slaves and has his child, much to her white husband's shock. The baby is sold, and twenty years later is unknowingly purchased by his white mother, who now runs the plantation. A pending slave insurrection serves as a catalyst for her realization of the horrible truth, which she reveals to her son.

THE MONOLOGUE: At the top of the play, the prologue sets up the action for the final two acts. Amalia Jennings LeFarge (19 to 20) has been married against her will to a man she does not love (Louis), but she has continued her affair with the slave that she does love (Hector). Their love has produced a child. Because of the time, she must turn her child over to slave traders or risk his being killed by her insanely furious husband. She seeks to make her doctor understand the justification for the love she feels for her lover.

TIME AND PLACE: 1820. The Jennings Plantation, South Carolina. Amalia's bedroom.

AMALIA: When I came home from Charleston
    with my brand new dashing husband,
    Daddy had the slaves line the path
    from the gate to the front porch;
    and as we walked through the ranks
    each one stepped up with
    the nosegays they had picked —
    awkward bunches of wildflowers.
    I was laughing, gathering up bouquets
    and tossing them to Louis.
    We were almost to the porch
    when suddenly there appeared this . . .

this rose. One red rose,
thrust right into the path so we had to stop.
I recognized him right away.
We hadn't seen each other
since Daddy sent him to the fields.
We used to sneak out to Mama's
old cutting garden; it was overgrown
and the roses had run particularly wild!
(Softly, remembering.)
One day he covered me in rose petals,
then blew them off, one by one.
He'd never seen anything like them
back in Africa.
(In wonder.)
And there he stood, all grown up,
with one red rose held out
like it was a piece of him
growing straight from his fist.
"What a lovely tribute to the bride!" I said —
(Shaking off the spell of the memory.)
then passed it to Louis to tuck in with the rest.
I made one mistake — Louis.
I don't have to go on living it.

THE DARKER FACE OF THE EARTH
by Rita Dove

American (Southern): Female

THE PLAY: In this retelling of the classic Greek tragedy, Rita Dove sets the *Oedipus* story on a South Carolina plantation in the antebellum (1820–1840) South. A white plantation owner's daughter has an affair with one of their slaves and has his child, much to her white husband's shock. The baby is sold, and twenty years later is unknowingly purchased by his white mother, who now runs the plantation. A pending slave insurrection serves as a catalyst for her realization of the horrible truth, which she reveals to her son.

THE MONOLOGUE: Phebe has been a slave on the Jennings Plantation since her birth. As a confidante and admirer of Augustus, she has been encouraged to participate in the insurrection. Augustus gets her to reveal the roots of her sorrow and the hardships that were unjustly visited upon her parents.

TIME AND PLACE: 1840. Early evening. The sitting room of Mrs. Amalia Jennings LaFarge on the Jennings Plantation, South Carolina.

[AUGUSTUS: And your folks?]
PHEBE: My father was sold before I was borned.
    Mama . . . it's a long story.
[AUGUSTUS: I got time.]
    (Phebe stares down at the ground as if she's conjuring the memory out of the dust; then she begins.)
PHEBE: Mama worked in the kitchen until
    I was about five; that's when
    fever broke out in the quarters.
    She used to set table scraps out
    for the field hands, and I
    stuck wildflowers in the baskets
    to pretty 'em up. Mama said
    you never know what a flower can mean
    to somebody in misery.

That fever tore through the cabins like wildfire.
Massa Jennings said the field hands
spread contamination and forbid them
to come near to the house, but
Mama couldn't stand watching them
just wasting away — so she started
sneaking food to the quarters at night.
Then the fever caught her, too.
She couldn't hide it long.
And Massa Jennings found out.
(Gulps a deep breath for strength, reliving the scene.)
Mama started wailing right there at the stove.
Hadn't she been a good servant?
Who stayed up three nights straight
to keep Massa's baby girl among the living
when her own mother done left this world?
Who did he call when the fire
needed lighting? Who mended the pinafores
Miss Amalia was forever snagging on bushes?
Mama dropped to her knees
and stretched out her arms along the floor.
She didn't have nowheres to go;
she'd always been at the Big House.
"Where am I gonna lay
my poor sick head?" she asked.
He stood there, staring
like she was a rut in the road,
and he was trying to figure out
how to get around it.
Then he straightened his waistcoat
and said: "You have put me and my child
in the path of mortal danger,
and you dare ask me what to do
with your nappy black head?"
He didn't even look at her —
just spoke off into the air
like she was already a ghost.
(Woodenly.)
She died soon after.

THE DAYS AND NIGHTS OF BEEBEE FENSTERMAKER
by William Snyder

American (Southern): Female

THE PLAY: Set in an American city with definite Southern leanings, the play follows the life of the ambitious, but ultimately unfulfilled Beebee Fenstermaker. Beebee has just graduated from college, and instead of living in her old hometown, waiting for life to happen to her, she decides to move up to the city and become an author. After her savings run out, she is forced to take a nine-to-five job and watch her passionate ambitions slowly slip away — the victim of a lack of drive, talent, and miscellaneous heartbreaks along the way.

THE MONOLOGUE: Beebee (20 to 24) has just moved into her new apartment in the city and is making a new friend. As she begins her new life, she is filled with the exhilaration of possibilities and spills out her life story to her helpful new neighbor, Nettie Jo.

TIME AND PLACE: Beebee's apartment. An American city (in the South?). Early evening. Present.

BEEBEE: I guess so. I had to get out, though. My family life was very complicated. It's funny. On the one hand I believe my future's as bright as a button and nothin' can stand in my way. But sometimes when I'm home, a little devil gets next to me and says, "Beebee, you fly mighty high in your mind's eye, honey. But if you ever took the trouble to look two inches past your nose you'd see your life was signed, sealed, and delivered before you were born. And it's got nothin' to do with love or careers or flights of fancy." In one way or another my whole family's just waitin' it out. They talk about what they're gonna do or what they should have done but they're just sittin' there waitin' for the axe to fall. And I must say, when I walk those streets in the dead of August, and the trees are dry as paper and the grass is burnt up crisp. And the sun's so hot and the air's so thick they shut out all the sounds. And I go to my grandmother's and see her movin' from room to room, doin' a little dab here and a little dab there. Waitin' for night to come so she can sit on the porch and do something that's *nothin'*. I think there's no comfort on this porch. There's no life in this town. There's no hope in this world. And God has long since passed away. Fall in line, Beebee, fall in line. In a hundred years who'll know the difference. Follow the path of least resistance, act out your part and *die*. But I said no! *(Crosses to bureau.)* I'm not gonna sit around waitin' for what I dread most to happen to me. I'm not gonna be one more ribbon on the maypole. *(Sets bureau.)* I'm cuttin' loose! So last week when I got home from college — before I could even give myself time to think — I cashed in my six hundred dollars worth of savin's bonds I'd received over the years as prize money — packed up Miss Amelia Earhart — *(Gets other suitcase and places it upstage of bureau.)* and high-tailed it down to the Trailways Bus Station and took off. So here I am, footloose and ready to tackle anything. I got money, an apartment, and I'm free!

EARLY DARK
by Reynolds Price

American (Southern): Female

THE PLAY: Set in North Carolina in 1957, *Early Dark* traces the journey of love taken by Rosacoke Mustian and the man who tortures her mind, Wesley Beavers. As she struggles with deciding the path of her life and the illogical nature of affection, Rosacoke endures the callous nature of her family, the seeming insensitivity of her object of affection, and the cruel accidents of nature.

THE MONOLOGUE: Rosacoke (20) traces the roots of her obsession with Wesley back to one special day as she talks to her mama.

TIME AND PLACE: July 1957. Late afternoon. North Carolina. Rosacoke's house.

ROSACOKE: *(Still at the window, facing out; realizing as she goes.)* Seven years this November. You had punished me for laughing that morning in church, and I wanted to die — which was nothing unusual — but guessed I could live if I breathed a little air, so I picked up a bucket and walked to the woods to hunt some nuts and win you back. It was getting on late. I was hoping you were worried. I was past Mr. Isaac's in the really deep woods. The leaves were all gone, but I hadn't found a nut. Still I knew of one tree Mildred Sutton had showed me — I was headed for that — and I found it finally. It was loaded — pecans the size of sparrows — and in the top fork a boy, a stranger to me. He was not even scared. He seemed to live there, twenty yards off the ground, staring out dead-level. I said "Are you strong enough to shake your tree?" — "If I wanted to," he said. I said "Well, want to please; I'm standing here hungry." He thought and then braced his long legs and arms and rocked four times — pecans nearly killed me. I rummaged round and filled my bucket, my pockets. He had still not faced me; so I said "Don't you want to share some of my pecans?" Then he looked down and smiled and said "I heard they were God's." I said "No, really they belong to Mr. Isaac Alston. He can't see this far." — "I can see him," he said. "You may can see Philadelphia," I said — he was looking back north — and he nodded to that but didn't look down. "How old are you?" I said. He said "Fifteen" and shut up again. "I'm thirteen," I said. He said, "You'll live" and smiled once more toward Philadelphia and I came on home. I wanted him then and every day since.

GRACELAND
by Ellen Byron

American (Southern): Female

THE PLAY: In this short play, an obsession over Elvis brings two total strangers to an intimate knowledge of each other as they wait for the gates of Graceland to open up.

THE MONOLOGUE: The author describes Rootie (22) as being "from a tiny town outside of Lafayette, Louisiana, Cajun country. She has a frail build, with an almost childlike body. From a distance, she could pass for thirteen. She is uneducated and extremely simple, naive, and unworldly. She could almost be mistaken for being somewhat slow-witted, but she isn't. Her lack of education and experience have made her very innocent and trusting. Having grown up surrounded by men, she is unsure of how to act with women but wants very much to be liked." In this scene, she is trying to explain her reasons for coming to Elvis's grave, and how the memory of her dead brother, Beau, inspires her to have hope in her tragedy of a life.

TIME AND PLACE: June 4, 1982, three days before Elvis Presley's mansion, Graceland, is to be opened to the public for the first time. 5 AM.

ROOTIE: Stop, please — (*Bev lets go. Rootie takes a breath. Removes wig and clutches it in her hand with other possessions.*) Well — where we live in Luziana is a real small town kind of near the Gulf. We're cajun folks. Beau's real name was Beaufils. Know what that means?

Beautiful son. Beaufils.

Well, everybody's been there a while, so we all pretty much know each other. The guys are all good buddies and do stuff together —

Anyway, about a month ago, right down the street from us, some guys who work on one of the oil rigs off the gulf took a house. And one of the guys was named Drew. And the funny thing about Drew was that he looked so much like Beau. I know I wasn't just seeing things, because Weebo noticed too, and they got real close. They'd go hunt or fish the bayou and we'd have dinner, all three of us. It was real nice.

(*She stops.*)

Well, Weebo had to make a run up to Shreveport for a week, but Drew kept coming around. We'd go for walks, or just sit and talk sometimes. Then I noticed something real strange — Beau used to kind of turn his head sideways like this *(Shows Bev.)* when he asked you a question. One day Drew was asking me something and he did the exact same thing, turned his head just that way. Gave me prickles on my arm. That's when I decided I would share my most special place with him. See, I got this special place that Beau used to take me to. I never been there with anyone else, even Weebo. But I had to be 100 percent sure I could share it with Drew, so I said, "Drew, who is your absolute most favorite hero who ever was?"

[BEV: And when he said Elvis, you knew.]

ROOTIE: Like in a vision or something. So last night I got all dressed up and at midnight, I took Drew there. About a mile from us is this dirt road. And if you follow it, you come to two long lines of the most beautiful trees you ever seen, with a big wide alley between them. And you follow this alley for a ways, thinking you'll come to something real neat at the end. But all there is is a field. It's where a plantation was about a hundred years ago, but it burnt down and now all that's left is the alley of trees. When I was little, Beau used to take me there late at night, put me on his shoulders and run down the alley. And sometimes we'd dance in all the quiet and dark, just Beau and me. When Drew and me got there, all the stars were out and it was just like I was little again. Everything was so beautiful. But then I saw that there were these people down on the field having a picnic or something. I didn't want to go, but Drew pulled my arm and said to come on. Then I saw who it was. It was Weebo and all his friends.

[BEV: But how did they know where it was?]

ROOTIE: Drew told them. See, Weebo told Drew I had this place I always went off to by myself and he was just dying to know where it was. Drew bet him 50 dollars that he could find out all about it. Weebo was so mad at me. Kept yelling that I cost him 50 bucks and I was just another stupid tramp.

[BEV: Poor thing.]

ROOTIE: It wasn't just that. They'd all been drinking a while, I guess, and Weebo was real drunk. He grabbed me hard and yelled to all the other guys, "You wanna see what Drew could've ended up with?" Then he poured beer onto a napkin, grabbed my face, and began scrubbing off all my makeup. He just kept scrubbing and pouring, and my face got all red and scratchy, my hair got all wet, my clothes were just fulla beer. Then he stood me right in the middle of everyone and said, "Now, Rootie, you gotta walk all the way home through the center of town just the way you are. I want to be sure everyone can see the real Rootie Mallert for once." So I walked home, all fulla beer, then I washed myself, took my kitchen money, and left. I had to. I couldn't face anyone again after what they seen. And my special place was gone, it was like it burnt down all over again.

[BEV: How much money have you got?]

ROOTIE: I got about 30 dollars. And my favorite pillow. See, Bev, where I come from, everybody's always putting together special things so they can touch God, charms and stuff. So I figured if I came here right at this special time, everything must come together, like Beau's birthday, and the house opening, and maybe I could touch — *(Rootie trails off. Pause.)*

THE TRESTLE AT POPE LICK CREEK
by Naomi Wallace

American (Southern): Female

THE PLAY: A coming of age play about the unique, complicated, and ultimately tragic relationship between two teenagers, *The Trestle at Pope Lick Creek,* follows the journey of Dalton Chance and Pace Creagan as they discover the trials and joys of puberty.

THE MONOLOGUE: Pace Creagan (17) likes to play chicken with the train that passes over Pope Lick Creek. She runs the trestle toward the oncoming train and jumps off the track just as the train begins to cross the trestle — at least, that's how it's supposed to happen. She's spent the past few months training her new friend, Dalton, for their impending run across the trestle, and they've become quite close. She confronts him with the truth behind the tragic death of the *last* friend she ran the trestle with — Brett Weaver.

TIME AND PLACE: Under the trestle at the dried-up Pope Lick Creek. 1936. A town outside a city somewhere in the United States.

PACE: *(Beat.)* But you were wrong the other day. That's not what a train does to you. It doesn't much mush you up in neat little pieces. This train. She's a knife. That's why we loved her. Me and Brett. This train, you've seen her. So much beauty she's breathless: a huge hunk and chunk of shiny black coal blasted fresh out of the mountain. *(Beat.)* We had a good start. Me and Brett. We both could of made it. 'Course Brett, he was faster. I expected to be running behind. But Brett was worried. About me. He was stupid like that. He turned to look over his shoulder at me and he tripped. I thought he'd just jump up and keep going so I passed him right by. We'd timed it tight, and right then that engine was so close I could smell her. *(Beat.)* I thought Brett was right behind me. I thought he was running behind me. I could hear him behind me. He didn't call out. He didn't say wait up. I didn't know. Why didn't he call out? *(There is the real sound of a whistle in the distance.)* Not even a sound. Brett just sat there where he'd fallen. And then he stood up, slowly, like he had the time. He stood there looking at her, looking her straight in the face. Almost like it was a dare. Like: Go ahead and hit me. You can't do that to a train. You can't dare a train to hit you. 'Cause it will.

(Another whistle, closer this time.)

Just stood there like she could pass right through him for all he cared. Like he wasn't going to flinch.

(Dalton takes her arm.)

WOMEN OF MANHATTAN
by John Patrick Shanley

American (Southern): Female

THE PLAY: Set in New York, *Women of Manhattan* traces the lives and adventures of three best friends as they try to make sense of being independent women in the big city.

THE MONOLOGUE: Rhonda Louise (28) "hails from the Deep South, speaks and moves in a very deliberate way, and is slender and slow to react . . . she is, by nature, always a trifle weary and a trifle solemn, or very weary and very solemn." At her dinner party with her girlfriends, Rhonda attempts to explain why there is a pair of ratty, red sneakers still sitting near her wall.

TIME AND PLACE: Rhonda's apartment, Manhattan, New York. Late evening. The present.

RHONDA: I guess my big mistake was I revealed myself to him. That's where I really went wrong. You know, that thing that most people can't do? That thing that's supposed to be like the hardest thing to get to with another person? It took me time, but I struggled and strove and succeeded at last in revealing my innermost, my most personal soul to him.
[BILLIE: And what is that?]
[RHONDA: Never you mind.]
[JUDY: And what did he do?]
RHONDA: Nothing. Zip. Nothing. He just sat there with a coke in his hand like he was watching television, waiting for the next thing. Like that was a nice stop on the way to WHAT I CAN'T IMAGINE! The whole thing with him was such a letdown. But why am I surprised? You know? I mean, here I was congratulating myself on being able to show myself, show my naked self to a man. But what's the achievement? I chose to show myself to a wall. Right? That's why I was able to do it. He was a wall and I was really alone, showing myself to nobody at all. How much courage does that take? Even when I got it together to throw him out, and I made this speech at him and got all pink in the face and noble as shit. He just said all right and left. What did I delude myself into think-

ing was going on between us if that's how he could take it ending? "All right. Just lemme get my tools together, Rhonda Louise, and I'll get on to the next thing." You know how in that one school a thought you're the only thing real in the world, and everything else is just a dream? All these people and things, the stars in the sky, are just sparks and smoke from your own lonely fire in a big, big night. I always thought what a lotta intellectual nonsense that was until Jerry. I mean, to tell you the naked truth, I'm not even sure there was a Jerry. It seems impossible to me that there was. Sometimes I think I just got overheated, worked myself into a passion, and fell in love with that wall right there. It must've been! It must've been that wall and me, crazy, loving it cause I needed to love. And not a human man. I couldn't have poured everything out to a really truly human man, and him just stand there, and take it, and give nothing back. It's not possible. But when I get too far gone in that direction of thinking — and alone here some nights I do — at those times it does me good to look and see these sneakers there sitting on the floor. His sneakers. He was here. It happened.

A BIRD OF PREY
by Jim Grimsley

American (Southern): Male

THE PLAY: Set in an urban environment, *Bird of Prey* takes a harsh, grim view of the dangers that plague and tempt the lives of today's teens. Centered around the story of Monty and his family's turbulent move from Louisiana, the cruelties of peer pressure are given a stark twist in this drama.

THE MONOLOGUE: Evan (16) is new to town and is having problems adjusting to his new environment. The situation at home has not changed for the better, the way they all had hoped it would, and Evan is angry.

TIME AND PLACE: Afternoon. Outside a school in an urban environment. The present day.

NOTE: The terms *Mama* and *Daddy* are a Southern thing and should not be changed or cause any discomfort in the actor.

Monty exits slowly, in darkness. Angel follows him out. Lights rise elsewhere on Evan, facing the audience.

EVAN: I hate them for bringing us here. I hate Mama as much as I hate Daddy, and I hate Daddy all the time. I hate him when he sits around the house in his stinking tee shirt spilling beer all over everything and throwing up in the toilet. I hate the look in Mama's eyes when I'm at home, I hate the way she hides. This place stinks and she knows it and he knows it and they act like it's going to be different someday but it never will, and they know that too, they know they're lying and we shouldn't have come here, they know it will never get better here, but they won't take us home, I know they won't, they'll just sit here, and Daddy will keep getting drunk all the time because his job stinks and Mama will keep crying because he drinks so much and because we don't have any money, and they'll fight all night and we'll have to listen, me and Monty and Marie, we'll have to lay in that stinking apartment and listen to him screaming at her and her begging him to go to sleep.

Begging him not to hit her. I know. Things can never get better here, not for us. And they ought to know it and do something about it, they ought to take us home, but they won't. So I hate them almost as much as I hate this place. It's all I can feel, this ball of hate that's on fire, that's right here inside me all the time. It's all I can feel, till sometimes I wish I could just go away somewhere. Some place where I'd never have to think about anything again.

(Evan comes down from the platform as Marie enters from another direction.)

BLESSED ASSURANCE
by Laddy Sartin

American (Southern): Male

THE PLAY: A white café owner, Harlan, struggles with his conscience as his black waitress (and longtime family friend and nurse), Olivia, becomes an outspoken crusader for the right to vote. It's the summer of 1964, and in the Deep South, the right to vote for African-Americans is a heated issue. As Olivia continues her quest for the vote, her admirer Lewis and Harlan both try their separate but similar approaches to get her to drop her crusade. Even the threats by Slick, the troubled white café customer, are ineffectual as Olivia sets her sights on change.

THE MONOLOGUE: Slick (18 to 22) returns home for the first time in years and walks right into a race issue in his racist Southern small town. As he tries to reconnect with Harlan he (unknowingly perhaps?) poetically voices the bigoted beliefs of his townsfolk while telling of a special memory he has of his ship-working days.

TIME AND PLACE: Harlan's café. Summer, 1964. Deep South.

SLICK: I was on a crew boat out in the middle of the Gulf of Mexico. We carried food and stuff back and forth out to the drilling rigs.

Salt water as far as you can see in any direction.

See something strange every day. Never know what to expect offshore.

We used to see falling stars at night, see 'em by the thousands.

I saw the moon go down once just as the sun was coming up.

Together they turned the water all golden. When all of a sudden there were porpoises all around, in every direction. I mean just as sudden as a blink of the eye, any way you looked just as far as you could see, there was porpoises. Three or four of 'em dancing up on the tips of their tails, backwards. How can they do that? Dance backwards out across the top of the water? Oh Harlan, you never seen such. They was big striped ones and little spotted babies. They'd come up out of the water a dozen at a time and do these wild flips and dives. I swear it was porpoises all over the place. The Captain just shut the motors off and we got out on the bow of the boat and just watched. Old Captain laughed and said real quiet, like it was a secret, wouldn't it sure be something, that if when we die we don't go up to heaven but out to the Gulf of Mexico? Ah, he just got all tickled at himself and laughed. He said that was it, when he died he wanted to go to Heaven in the Gulf of Mexico and be a porpoise dancing in the streets of gold. And then we saw, not ten feet from the port side of us, a floatin' monkey. Yeah. A baboon. One of them they keep in cages at the zoo. It was floatin' face down. The Old Captain hollered, Look boy Look! It's one of them kind with the big ole red and yellow purple butts. He pointed and I saw it. He just snorted. Said that baboon was probably chasing them porpoises down the streets of gold and drowned. What a shame. That old baboon should know God ain't gonna let no monkey into the streets of heaven. *(Huge blast of steam. The hot water heater begins rattling its pipes.)*

BLESSED ASSURANCE
by Laddy Sartin

American (Southern): Male

THE PLAY: A white café owner, Harlan, struggles with his conscience as his black waitress (and longtime family friend and nurse), Olivia, becomes an outspoken crusader for the right to vote. It's the summer of 1964, and in the Deep South, the right to vote for African-Americans is a heated issue. As Olivia continues her quest for the vote, her admirer Lewis and Harlan both try their separate but similar approaches to get her to drop her crusade. Even the threats by Slick, the troubled white café customer, are ineffectual as Olivia sets her sights on change.

THE MONOLOGUE: Using the language of the time, Slick (18 to 22) has become more than the benign threat he originally appeared to be. He comes to Olivia as a representative of the hatred in the town and attempts to silence her.

TIME AND PLACE: Harlan's café. Summer, 1964. Deep South.

SLICK: Come on over here so you can hear me. Take all day, ain't nothing gonna change. Are you listening to me? Hey? Come on. *(Olivia at kitchen door.)* I been sent here to tell you how things are gonna be. In my heart I don't want none of this. You know that, don't you? You know why they sent me? Huh? Well, what? You ain't got nothing to say? Why couldn't you just stay in your place? You never done nothing like this before. Most folks, people in town, always thought of you as good colored. You know what they saying now, you know what the word is out on you? That you been listening to outside agitators. You stand there and stare at me like I done wrong, but it's you! It was you! You don't know your place. What would you think if I drove out to the country club and stood around knocking on the front door whining about somebody letting me in? They ain't gonna let me be no member of the country club. You see what I mean? What if I drove over to the Jews' synagogue and tried to get in? Ain't no way they gonna let me in, 'cause they know and I know I ain't no Jew. It ain't my place. So what in God's name do you think you doing romping around the courthouse? Huh?

[OLIVIA: Is that all you got to say?]

SLICK: [No that ain't all I got to say.] You think this is funny? I been sent here! I was forced to come. I was sent with a special message for you. I didn't want to let Harlan hear it, it'd just get him all upset.

For what you did yesterday . . . certain people around town, well . . . they say they gonna make you suffer.

They told me . . . if you ever go around the courthouse again . . . they said they'd drown you. You hear me! They said they'd drown you in your own blood! *(Olivia watches Slick for a moment then turns and goes back into the kitchen softly humming an old gospel song. Sally appears at back screen door.)* And you can cut out all that singing and stuff! Olivia!

CURSE OF THE STARVING CLASS
by Sam Shepard

American (Southern): Male

THE PLAY: A surreal exploration of a twisted family and their relationships with each other, *Curse of the Starving Class* is a dark study of the lives of a poor, rural family. As the father drinks the farm away, and the mother schemes to sell it and move to Europe, the daughter tries to rise above her shallow roots as her brother begins his walk down the same path as his father.

THE MONOLOGUE: Wesley's (16 to 18) father came home drunk again in the middle of the night and tore the front door off its hinges. His mother called the police and had him taken away. Wesley describes the dream he had while all the excitement was going on outside.

TIME AND PLACE: A farm (not necessarily in the South). The kitchen. Morning.

They look at each other for a moment. Ella breaks it by putting the bacon and bread down on top of the stove. Wesley goes back to cleaning up the debris. He keeps talking as Ella looks though the lower drawers of the stove and pulls out a frying pan. She lights one of the burners on the stove and starts cooking the bacon.

WESLEY: *(As he throws wood into wheelbarrow.)* I was lying there on my back. I could smell the avocado blossoms. I could hear the coyotes. I could hear stock cars squealing down the street. I could feel myself in my bed in my room in this house in this town in this state in this country. I could feel this country close like it was part of my bones. I could feel the presence of all the people outside, at night, in the dark. Even sleeping people I could feel. Even all the sleeping animals. Dogs. Peacocks. Bulls. Even tractors sitting in the wetness, waiting for the sun to come up. I was looking straight up at the ceiling at all my model airplanes hanging by all their thin metal wires. Floating. Swaying very quietly like they were being blown by someone's breath. Cobwebs moving with them. Dust laying on their wings. Decals peeling off their wings. My P-39. My Messerschmitt. My Jap Zero. I could feel myself lying far below them on my bed like I was on the ocean and overhead they were on reconnais-sance. Scouting me. Floating. Taking pictures of the enemy. Me, the enemy. I could feel the space around me like a big, black world. I listened like an animal. My listening was afraid. Afraid of sound. Tense. Like any second something could invade me. Some foreigner. Something indescribable. Then I heard the Packard coming up the hill. From a mile off I could tell it was the Packard by the sound of the valves. The lifters have a sound like nothing else. Then I could picture my Dad driving it. Shifting unconsciously. Downshifting into second for the last pull up the hill. I could feel the headlights closing in. Cutting through the orchard. I could see the trees being lit one after the other by the lights, then going back to black. My heart was pounding. Just from my Dad coming back. Then I heard him pull the brake. Lights go off. Key's turned off. Then a long silence. Him just sitting in the car. Just sitting. I picture him just sitting. What's he doing? Just sitting. Waiting to get out. Why's he waiting to get out? He's plastered and can't move. He's plastered and doesn't want to move. He's going to sleep there all night. He's slept there before. He's woken up with dew on the hood before. Freezing headache. Teeth covered with peanuts. Then I hear the door of the Packard open. A pop of metal. Dogs barking down the road. Door slams. Feet. Paper bag being tucked under one arm. Paper bag covering "Tiger Rose." Feet coming. Feet walking toward the door. Feet stopping. Heart pounding. Sound of door not opening. Foot kicking door. Man's voice. Dad's voice. Dad calling Mom. No answer. Foot kicking. Foot kicking harder. Wood splitting. Man's voice. In the night. Foot kicking hard through the door. One foot right through door. Bottle crashing. Glass breaking. Fist through door. Man cursing. Man going insane. Feet and hands tearing. Head smashing. Woman screaming. Mom screaming. Mom screaming for police. Man throwing wood. Man throwing up. Mom calling cops. Dad crashing away. Back down driveway. Car door slamming. Ignition grinding. Wheels screaming. First gear grinding. Wheels screaming off down hill. Packard disappearing. Sound disappearing. No sound. No sight. Planes still hanging. Heart still pounding. No sound. Mom crying soft. Soft crying. Then no sound. Then softly crying. Then moving around through house. Then no moving. Then crying softly. Then stopping. Then, far off the freeway could be heard.

(Wesley picks up one end of the wheelbarrow. He makes the sound of a car and pushes it off right, leaving Ella alone at the stove watching the bacon.)

THE DARKER FACE OF THE EARTH
by Rita Dove

American (Southern): Male

THE PLAY: In this retelling of the classic Greek tragedy, Rita Dove sets the *Oedipus* story on a South Carolina plantation in the antebellum (1820–1840) South. A white plantation owner's daughter has an affair with one of their slaves and has his child, much to her white husband's shock. The baby is sold and twenty years later is unknowingly purchased by his white mother, who now runs the plantation. The pending slave insurrection serves as the catalyst for the realization of the horrible truth which mother reveals to son.

THE MONOLOGUE: Augustus (20) is the newest slave on the plantation. Well-traveled and well-groomed by his former master, he has seen more of the world and all its possibilities than the rest of the Jennings' slaves. His words stir up the feelings of insurrection amongst the slaves as he begins to lead them to a freedom they never dreamed possible.

TIME AND PLACE: 1840. Noon. The field of Jennings Plantation, South Carolina.

AUGUSTUS: Santo Domingo, San Domingue, Hispaniola —
three names for an island
rising like a fortress
from the waters of the Caribbean.
An island of sun and forest,
wild fruit and mosquitoes —
and slaves, many slaves — half a million.
Slaves to chop sugar, slaves
to pick coffee beans, slaves to do
their French masters' every bidding.
Then one summer, news came
from the old country: Revolution!
Plantation owners broke into a sweat;
their slaves served cool drinks
while the masters rocked on their verandas,

discussing each outrage:
People marching against the king,
crowds pouring into the streets,
shouting three words:
Liberté!
Égalité!
Fraternité!
Liberté, Égalité, Fraternité — three words
were all the island masters talked about
that summer, while their slaves
served carefully and listened.
*(During the following speech, a smoldering growl among the slaves grows
louder and louder, until it explodes in a shout.)*
Black men meeting in a forest:
Eight days, they whispered,
and we'll be free. For eight days
bonfires flashed in the hills:
Equality. For eight days
tom-toms sang: Brothers and sisters.
And on the eighth day, swift as lightning,
the slaves attacked.
(Amalia enters, unseen, and stands listening.)
They came down the mountains
to the sound of tambourines and conch shells.
With torches they swept onto the plantations,
with the long harvest knives
they chopped white men down
like sugarcane. For three weeks
the flames raged; then the sun
broke through the smoke and shone
upon a new nation, a black nation —
Haiti!
(Looking intently at the faces around him.)
Now do you see
why they've kept this from us,
brothers and sisters?

THE DARKER FACE OF THE EARTH
by Rita Dove

American (Southern): Male

THE PLAY: In this retelling of the classic Greek tragedy, Rita Dove sets the *Oedipus* story on a South Carolina plantation in the antebellum (1820–1840) South. A white plantation owner's daughter has an affair with one of their slaves and has his child, much to her white husband's shock. The baby is sold, and twenty years later is unknowingly purchased by his white mother, who now runs the plantation. A pending slave insurrection serves as a catalyst for her realization of the horrible truth which she reveals to her son.

THE MONOLOGUE: His insurrection story overheard by Miss Amalia, Augustus (20) must report to her sitting room and entertain her with conversation. As she tries to catch him in his ignorance, Augustus responds with a metaphor about the nature and spirit of the people she considers to be weak and worthless.

TIME AND PLACE: 1840. Early evening. The sitting room of Mrs. Amalia Jennings LeFarge on the Jennings Plantation, South Carolina.

AUGUSTUS: *(Getting up from the floor.)* Now I have a story for you.
  Once there was a preacher slave
  went by the name of Isaac.
  When God called him
  he was a boy, out hunting rice birds.
  Killing rice birds is easy —
  just pinch off their heads.
  (Indicating the sherry.)
  May I?
  (Amalia flinches, nods. He pours the sherry expertly.)
  But one day, halfway up the tree
  where a nest of babies chirped,
  a voice called out: "Don't do it, Isaac."
  It was an angel, shining
  in the crook of a branch.

Massa let him preach.
What harm could it do?
(Sitting down in the damask chair.)
Then a slave uprising in Virginia
had all the white folks
watching their own niggers
for signs of treachery.
No more prayer meetings, Isaac!
But God would not wait,
so Isaac kept on preaching
at night, in the woods.
Of course he was caught.
Three of his congregation
were shot on the spot, three others branded
and their feet pierced.
But what to do about Isaac,
gentle Isaac who had turned traitor?
First they flogged him. Then
they pickled the wounds with salt water,
and when they were nearly healed,
he was flogged again, and the wounds
pickled again, and on and on for weeks
while Massa sold off Isaac's children
one by one. They took him to see
his wife on the auction block,
baby at her breast.
A week later it was his turn.
His back had finally healed;
but as his new owner led him
from the auction block,
Isaac dropped down dead.
(Pause; more to himself than to Amalia.)
They couldn't break his spirit,
so they broke his heart.
(They stare at each other for a moment; then Amalia rises and walks to the window. It has gotten dark outside.)

KILLER JOE
by Tracy Letts

American (Southern): Male

THE PLAY: A disturbing look into the lives of an extremely dysfunctional Texas family, *Killer Joe* reveals what happens when greed, lust, and immorality take root in the heart.

THE MONOLOGUE: Chris Smith (22) has hired Killer Joe to kill his mother, thinking that her $50,000 life insurance policy will take care of him and his sister for years to come. When Joe asks for Chris' sister as a retainer (a security payment of sorts until the life insurance policy is cashed) before he'll do the job, Chris reluctantly agrees to give her to Joe. After a week of Joe enjoying his sister's hospitality, Chris has a change of heart.

TIME AND PLACE: Chris's dad's trailer home on the outskirts of Dallas. Daytime. The present.

Lights rise: Daylight streams through the windows. Killer Joe sits at the kitchen table, listening to an evangelist on the radio. His gun lies on the table. T-Bone barks crazily. Pounding on the door. Joe lifts his gun, cocks it.

CHRIS: *(Offstage.)* Joe?! Joe?!
(Chris rushes in, sweating, out of breath, panicked. His head and hand are bruised, bandaged. Joe holsters his gun.)

Ah, thank God! I was afraid . . . I wouldn't get here, and . . . it'd be too late . . . ah, thank God . . .

Listen. We gotta stop this thing. We can't . . . *(Chris turns off the radio.)* I been in a lotta trouble, all my life, but I never tried nothin' like this before.

I'm sorry. I didn't mean to waste your time.

I hate that bitch. I've always hated her. I just . . . I can't be the one, y'know?

But more than that, the main thing, really, is, is, is Dottie. I mean, my sister . . . she never did nothin' to nobody, y'know? And for me to . . . I can't be . . . responsible.

And you can't have her. I can't let you have her. You gotta give her up, cause I can't look her in the eyes otherwise.

Do you understand Joe? I don't want my sister to see you again. I don't think you're a good influence.

I mean, come on, Joe, you kill people, for Chrissake. Y'know?

No offense. I mean, it's not like me and Dad or Mom have been especially good influences. But Dottie managed to turn out all right anyway. And it just seems like the best thing I can do for her now is to keep her away from people who won't do her any good.

So I think it'd be best if you and me just shook hands and forgot any of us ever met. Is that okay? Can't we just walk away from it before it goes too far? None of us are any better off, but we're really no worse off, either.

I'm no better off. I owe Digger Soames six thousand dollars. I'll never have that kind of money, not ever.

And, you know, even if I had it, wouldn't that suck, handin' it over to these guys? I'd wanna keep that money, try to make somethin' with it.

I tried startin' a farm once. That seemed like the kind of life I want. Workin' for myself, outside a lot, make my own hours, live in the country, smoke dope, watch TV. That's all I really want.

So I started a rabbit farm. I built the whole thing, by myself. I was livin' with a coupla guys out near Mesquite, but they didn't help me; I built it, with my own two hands. Lumber, chicken wire, water bottles, pellets. Rabbits. I loved those little bastards. They smell like shit, and they fuck all the time, but they're awful easy goin' animals.

I left for a coupla weeks, cause of this girl down in Corpus, and when I got back, a rat, or a skunk, or somethin' had got in the pen, and it was rabid. Awful hot out, too.

They just tore each other apart. Their eyes were rollin', and foamin' at the mouth, and . . . and screamin'. Did you know rabbits can scream? They sound just like little girls.

It was disturbing.

I started sellin' dope for a living. I knew more about it.

(Joe checks a beeper affixed to his belt, then goes to the door, looks outside.)

So I can't pay this guy, and I don't even really want to.

That means you gotta get out, Joe. You gotta get outta here, and leave my sister alone, forever. Otherwise, you and me're gonna have some trouble.

Do you understand?

Do you understand?

(A long silence. Chris slowly turns and looks at a large, overstuffed garbage bag sitting by the other garbage in the kitchen. Chris walks to the bag, starts to open it.)

THE PIANO LESSON
by August Wilson

American (Southern): Male

THE PLAY: Wilson's Pulitzer Prize–winning play examines the lives of an African-American family and their relationships to their prized family piano. When Boy Willie comes up from Mississippi to visit his sister in Pittsburgh, she knows that something is up. She's right. Boy Willie is scheming to sell his half of the treasured piano to raise funds to buy the land his family once worked as slaves. The piano was carved by their great-grandfather with intricate scenes of the history of their family, and Berniece (his sister) will never consent to let the piano go. The piano lesson is about more than music for this troubled family.

THE MONOLOGUE: Boy Willie (30) is finding his sister less than receptive about his idea to sell the piano, and he tries to reason with her.

TIME AND PLACE: Berniece's Uncle Doaker's house. Parlor. Late evening. Present.

BOY WILLIE: Now, I'm gonna tell you the way I see it. The only thing that make that piano worth something is them carvings Papa Willie Boy put on there. That's what make it worth something. That was my great-grandaddy. Papa Boy Charles brought that piano into the house. Now, I'm supposed to build on what they left me. You can't do nothing with that piano sitting up here in the house. That's just like if I let them watermelons sit out there and rot. I'd be a fool. All right now, if you say to me, Boy Willie, I'm using that piano. I give out lessons on it and that help me make my rent or whatever. Then that be something else. I'd have to go on and say, well, Berniece using that piano. She building on it. Let her go on and use it. I got to find another way to get Sutter's land. But Doaker say you ain't touched that piano the whole time it's been up here. So why you wanna stand in my way? See, you just looking at the sentimental value. See, that's good. That's all right. I take my hat off whenever somebody say my daddy's name. But I aint' gonna be no fool about no sentimental value. You can sit up here and look at the piano for the next hundred years and it's just gonna be a piano. You can't make more than that. Now I want to get Sutter's land with that piano. I get Sutter's land and I can go down and cash in the crop and get my seed. As long as I got the land and the seed then I'm all right. I can always get me a little something else. 'Cause that land give back to you. I can make me another crop and cash that in. I still got the land and the seed. But that piano don't put out nothing else. You ain't got nothing working for you. Now, the kind of man my daddy was he would have understood that. I'm sorry you can't see it that way. But that's why I'm gonna take that piano out of here and sell it.

THE PIANO LESSON
by August Wilson

American (Southern): Male

THE PLAY: Wilson's Pulitzer Prize–winning play examines the lives of an African-American family and their relationships to their prized family piano. When Boy Willie comes up from Mississippi to visit his sister in Pittsburgh, she knows that something is up. She's right. Boy Willie is scheming to sell his half of the treasured piano to raise funds to buy the land his family once worked as slaves. The piano was carved by their great-grandfather with intricate scenes of the history of their family, and Berniece (his sister) will never consent to let the piano go. The piano lesson is about more than music for this troubled family.

THE MONOLOGUE: Lymon (29) has come up to Pittsburgh with Boy Willie to help him sell watermelons. He has decided to stay in town and try his luck with work and women. After his first night on the town, he returns to Berniece's house with a different sense of the women he had held in such high regard. When Berniece asks him what they are like, he answers her.

TIME AND PLACE: Berniece's Uncle Doaker's house. Parlor. Late evening. Present.

LYMON: Mostly they be lonely and looking for somebody to spend the night with them. Sometimes it matters who it is and sometimes it don't. I used to be the same way. Now it got to matter. That's why I'm here now. Dolly liable not to even recognize me if she sees me again. I don't like women like that. I like my women to be with me in a nice and easy way. That way we can both enjoy ourselves. The way I see it we the only two people like us in the world. We got to see how we fit together. A woman that don't want to take the time to do that I don't bother with. Used to. Used to bother with all of them. Then I woke up one time with this woman and I didn't know who she was. She was the prettiest woman I have ever seen in my life. I spent the whole night with her and didn't even know it. I had never taken the time to look at her. I guess she kinda knew I ain't never really looked at her. She must have known that cause she ain't wanted to see me no more. If she had wanted to see me I believe we might have got married. How come you ain't married? It seem like to me you would be married. I remember Avery down home. I used to call him plain old Avery. Now he Reverend Avery. That's kinda funny about him becoming a preacher. I like when he told about how that come to him in a dream about them sheep people and them hobos. Nothing ever come to me in a dream like that. I just dream about women. Can't never seem to find the right one.

THE PIANO LESSON
by August Wilson

American (Southern): Male

THE PLAY: Wilson's Pulitzer Prize–winning play examines the lives of an African-American family and their relationships to their prized family piano. When Boy Willie comes up from Mississippi to visit his sister in Pittsburgh, she knows that something is up. She's right. Boy Willie is scheming to sell his half of the treasured piano to raise funds to buy the land his family once worked as slaves. The piano was carved by their great-grandfather with intricate scenes of the history of their family, and Berniece (his sister) will never consent to let the piano go. The piano lesson is about more than music for this troubled family.

THE MONOLOGUE: Boy Willie (30) has not stopped trying to get Berniece to sell the piano. He has come to the point where he will just sell it whether she gives him permission to or not. As Berniece does her daughter's hair, Boy Willie injects his opinions of her childrearing and how he would do things differently.

TIME AND PLACE: Berniece's Uncle Doaker's house. Parlor. Early evening. Present.

BOY WILLIE: What I want to bring a child into this world for? Why I wanna bring somebody else into all this for? I'll tell you this . . . If I was Rockefeller I'd have forty or fifty. I'd make one every day. Cause they gonna start out in life with all the advantages. I ain't got no advantages to offer nobody. Many is the time I looked at my daddy and seen him staring off at his hands. I got a little older I know what he was thinking. He sitting there saying, "I got these big old hands but what I'm gonna do with them? Best I can do is make a fifty-acre crop for Mr. Stovall. Got these big old hands capable of doing anything. I can take and build something with these hands. Unless I go out here and kill me somebody and take what they got . . . it's a long row to hoe for me to get something of my own. So what I'm gonna do with these big old hands? What would you do?"

See now . . . if he had his own land he wouldn't have felt that way. If he had something under his feet that belonged to him he could stand up taller. That's what I'm talking about. Hell, the land is there for everybody. All you got to do is figure out how to get you a piece. Ain't no mystery to life. You just got to go out and meet it square on. If you got a piece of land you'll find everything else fall right into place. You can stand right up next to the white man and talk about the price of cotton . . . the weather, and anything else you want to talk about. If you teach that girl that she living at the bottom of life, she's gonna grow up and hate you.

THE TRESTLE AT POPE LICK CREEK
by Naomi Wallace

American (Southern): Male

THE PLAY: A coming-of-age play about the unique, complicated, and ultimately tragic relationship between two teenagers, *The Trestle at Pope Lick Creek,* follows the journey of Dalton Chance and Pace Creagan as they discover the trials and joys of puberty.

THE MONOLOGUE: From his jail cell, Dalton (15) tries to explain the unique nature of his relationship with Pace to his mother.

TIME AND PLACE: Dalton's jail cell. 1936. A town outside a city somewhere in the United States.

DALTON: *(Shouts.)* I didn't hold her! *(Now he is quiet.)* She held me. Pace did. But it wasn't that. Holding. Sometimes when I was with her, she wasn't there. Or when I was without her, she was there, but not there. Alone at night in bed, I could feel her breath in my ears. No.

    That's not it.

    It was something more. Like at school. At school they teach you. To speak. They say it's math, geometry, whatever. But they're teaching you to speak. Not about the world but about things. Just things: a door, a map.

[PACE: A cup. Just the name of it.]

DALTON: Not what a cup means, who picked it up, who drank from it,

[PACE: who didn't and why;]

DALTON: where a map came from, who fixed in the rivers, who'll take the wrong turn; or a door. Who cut the wood and hung it there? Why that width, that height? And who made that decision? Who agreed to it? Who didn't?

    They just teach us to speak the things. So that's what we speak. But there's no past that way.

    And no future.

    'Cause after you've said the thing, you move on. You don't look back. You never think to cross it, never stop and turn.

    She laughed at everything that seemed right.

It wasn't just at night. In the day sometimes. Not her voice but the sound of her. I could hear it. Like water running in a pipe. Coal shifting in the grate. But that's not it. It was more like this. This cup. *(Dalton takes his drinking cup, calmly kneels, and breaks it on the floor. His hand bleeds slightly. He sorts through the pieces.)* Look. This was sand and heat. Not long ago. Other things, too. Pieces and bits. And now. It's something else. Glass. Blood. And it's broken. *(He picks up a large piece, nears Gin.)* I could cut you open with it. *(Gin slaps him in the face. He's taken aback, put in his place.)*

But that's what she did to me. Cut me open and things weren't just things after that. They were more. What they'd once been and what they could be besides. I was just a kid —

I never even thought about it. But then one day I wasn't sure. She did that to me. She made me — hesitate. In everything I did. I was. Unsure. Look. It's not a cup anymore; it's a knife.

(Pace stands close to Dalton, but he cannot see her.)

APPENDIX

CLASSROOM EXERCISES

BRITISH (STANDARD AND COCKNEY) EXERCISES

British Experts/Cockney Talk Show   On a talk show (especially fun with a Cockney host), two people speaking Standard English are both experts on the same subject but have opposing views; for example, in a show with "rock" experts, one is a legitimate geologist and the other an animator who creates rocks on a computer for such films as *Jurassic Park*. The audience of the talk show is made up of Cockney speakers. The host keeps the conversation going and occasionally allows the audience to participate. Audience members pick a favorite guest and target the other with insulting, banal questions.

Smelly-Sexy-Funny   This is a popular theater exercise that can be used with any dialect, but it works well with Standard British. Four people participate: one person is the host of a party; the other three are the guests. Before the exercise starts, each person silently chooses one person onstage who is "smelly," another who is "sexy," and a third who is "funny." He or she endows these people with his or her choices in a subtle way throughout the scene. After each person has decided (without telling anyone else) who is who, everyone but the host leaves the set. The host mimes setting up for the party. One by one, the guests arrive and are affected by the presence of their smelly-sexy-funny people. The teacher can side-coach by saying make your smelly 100 times more smelly, etc. Each guest will find a reason to leave on his or her own. Afterwards, quiz the audience to find out who was who to each of the actors.

Character Interviews   Two people interview each other in dialect and find out where each other is from, what he or she does, what he or she likes, etc. The interview should be completely spontaneous and will help the actors find the natural cadence of their characters, as well as helping them remember what they learned about the region where their dialect originates. It can be repeated throughout the rehearsal process. Partners are not necessary; the actor could interview him- or herself, aloud.

Character Dream   This personal exercise may need outside coaching. After researching a given dialect, including looking at photos, reading newspaper articles, watching films, and more, the actor goes to a quiet place, closes his or her eyes, and "sees" a place in the country/region being studied. The actor should look for specific details, like the color of the paint that is peeling off the side of an old wooden building. The actor continues to daydream about this place, seeing the people around the area, what they are wearing, how they are walking, etc. He or she then adds the sense of touch and smell, such as sensing what the weather is like. At a certain point in the daydream, the actor must catch a glimpse of him- or herself in a reflective object and see what body type has come to mind. The actor looks for specific details and asks him- or herself: What am I wearing? How do I feel today? As the image becomes stronger, the actor may want to get up and move around the room, allowing the character's body to enter his or her body. After a short time, the voice of the character can reveal itself (in dialect of course), and the actor can begin to talk aloud to whoever is around. If no one is around, the actor can create an imaginary interview and proceed in an improvised monologue.

Character Walk   This exercise does not have to be done quickly; it may take about fifteen to twenty minutes. The teacher asks the students to first walk normally, then to adopt a variety of other walking styles. Following are suggested directions for these various character walks. (This exercise was adapted from a Laban method exercise.)

Without talking, walk around the room the way you normally walk. As you walk, keep your eyes and head up and active. Now walk a bit quicker and see how that changes your thoughts. Now go back to neutral walking. Now walk as if you were walking through very thick mud that covered you up to your chin. Now go back to neutral. Now walk as if you were walking in zero gravity. Now go back to neutral. Walk as if all your moves originated from your stomach. Now back to neutral. Change your center (where all your moves originate) to your toes and lead your walk with your toes. Now back to neutral. Now lead with your chin. Now back to neutral. Keep changing your center to find new ways to walk and constantly check in with what that walk does to your thoughts and sense of self. From neutral, walk with directness. Find a focus and directly go to it. Change direction and keep changing direction, but always with purpose. Then relax and go back to neutral. Now walk without purpose, try to commit, but then change your mind. What does that do to your body? Now go back to neutral. Walk around the room pigeon-toed. And back to neutral. Now walk bow-legged. And back to neutral. Walk as though you are completely bound in duct tape (keep moving); if you fall, try to get back up. And back to neutral. Walk as if every part of your body weighed 500 pounds. And back to neutral. Now, think of three of the ways you just walked (quickly, slowly, zero gravity, stomach-centered, toe-centered, chin-centered, directly, indirectly, pigeon-toed, bow-legged, bound, heavy) and put three of them together and walk around the room. Keep this walk up as you think about the voice that would come from this character (in dialect, of course). Think of this person's name, occupation, etc. Now find a partner and interview each other in these characters.

Irish Exercises

Galway Monologue   A member of the group gets an ordinary object from an audience member and sets it down on a chair. Then, one at a time, group members come to the chair, hold up the object, and sit down and talk about its relevance in their lives. The object may be a book, for example, but the monologist can make the object anything he or she wants (i.e., it can be a monologue about "this pack of gum I got on the Aran Islands"). Monologues should be done for authenticity in the Irish dialect — rhythm, inflection, and sound changes should be the focus — not necessarily for humor. The monologist finishes his or her story after about two minutes, and then sets the object back down on the chair, and another group member comes up to do a different monologue. The monologues are completely improvised. Group members do not have to add onto anyone's story, but reincorporation from an earlier monologue can be creative ("I got this jewelry box from my mom when I was three." And then, from a different person, "I was searching for the perfect gift for my daughter when I found this old jewelry box in my hope chest"). Everyone in the group should rotate through the exercise.

Irish Scene Without I/You   Players speak in their Irish dialect in a scene of their choice (no more than four people should be up at a time due to focus issues). In the course of the scene, no actor may say the words *I, me, my, myself, mine, you, your, yourself,* or *yours.* With this restriction, people will slow down and become creative in their expression. If a player says one of the forbidden words, he or she must leave the scene gracefully, and another member of the class can join in until everyone has been onstage at least once.

Limerick Line   The students line up and, following the pattern of a limerick poem, make up a limerick. The first person in line says the first line of the limerick, the second person continues the limerick, and so on. The rhyming pattern for a limerick is AA BB A. Below is an example of the limerick rhythm.

> There once was a man from Manhattan.
> He had lots of rugs made from satin
> One day someone slipped
> And totally tripped
> (and) his face was suddenly flattened!

(Plus other previously mentioned exercises.)

RUSSIAN EXERCISES

Russian Translation   Two people sit facing each other, while two others stand behind them. The two people standing should maintain completely blank expressions on their faces throughout the improvisation. The two people sitting converse in Russian-accented gibberish. After Russian A (sitting) speaks, Translator A (standing) translates what he or she said into English but with a Russian accent. Then Russian B (sitting) responds in gibberish, and Translator B (standing) translates, and so on. After the scene has ended or been resolved, the sitters and standers switch places and repeat.

Russian Gibberish Warm-Up   The students stand in a circle. One student tosses a ball to a classmate and says a "Russian" word — not a *real* Russian word, just sounds that mimic Russian sounds. The catcher of the ball repeats the "word," and then throws the ball to someone else, saying a different Russian word. The ball toss can be continued for as long as desired. The faster the game goes, the better; do not try to be perfect in this one — it's gibberish!

Russian/Gibberish/Russian   In this exercise, the teacher/director uses a bell to control the language of the actors as they improvise a scene. The actors start out speaking English with a Russian accent. When the bell rings, they must switch to speaking gibberish, or vice versa. Each time the bell rings, the actors switch into whatever vocal direction they are not doing (either gibberish or Russian-accented English). The switch can happen in mid-sentence and should be as flawless and committed as possible.

(Plus other previously mentioned exercises.)

AMERICAN (NEW YORK) EXERCISES

Brooklyn Bench   This is a rotation exercise. One person sits on a bench; another person enters and strikes up a conversation in a Brooklyn accent — defining their relationship and a need. The first person finds a reason to leave (relatively quickly, keep them short), and the second person remains. A new person enters and strikes up a conversation and develops a relationship that could be completely unrelated. The second person finds a reason to leave, etc. The whole group rotates through the exercise, ending with the person who started sitting on the bench re-entering and ending the scene.

One-Minute Ramble   Students stand in a circle and take turns talking aloud for one full minute, trying to avoid pauses or self-censuring. In a Brooklyn (or any) accent, they may talk about anything that comes to mind. The sentences do not have to be connected; they can ramble about anything. This is a great exercise for figuring where and how students hold their tension and insecurities.

Brooklyn Standing/Sitting/Kneeling   This is another theater exercise that combines the physical lives of the actors with their emotional and verbal lives. Three actors are in this scene. At all times, one actor is sitting, one kneeling, and one standing. The actors can move around, but there can never be two people in the same position at the same time. To keep it interesting and raise the stakes, the audience can give verbal cues (such as groaning or going *oooo*) when two people are in the same position. If two people are caught in the same position for longer than fifteen seconds, their scene is done, and the next group goes up. It is important to keep the narrative going and the character relationships clear.

(Plus other previously mentioned exercises.)

American (Southern) Exercises

Southern New Choice   This exercise is controlled by the teacher. Two students get up to improvise a scene. When a person makes an offer ("That's a mighty fine *hat* you're wearing"), the teacher can call out "new choice" and the actor must (without hesitation or breaking character) make a new but related offer, for example: "That's a mighty fine *necklace* you're wearing." (new choice) "That's a mighty fine *belt* you're wearing." (new choice) "That's a mighty fine *purple felt overcoat* you're wearing." The teacher can stop saying "new choice" at any time, and the actor must then continue with the scene and accept what the final offer was. The teacher may call out "new choice" for either of the actors at any time, relating to any choice. This is especially useful in keeping the scenes positive and moving forward, such as: Actor A: "Do you want to dance with me?" Actor B: "No." (new choice) B: "Yes."

Southern Tag Monologue   One person stands and makes up a monologue on the spot (in a Southern accent, of course). When the next actor wants to take over, he or she simply walks up behind the first actor, taps him or her on the shoulder, and continues the monologue without pausing. The whole class takes turns continuing the monologue until the teacher decides it has ended, or it finds its end naturally.

Southern Subtext   This exercise requires some preparation. The teacher writes down subtext suggestions on pieces of paper (i.e., "I hate you" or "I'm afraid to tell you something") and puts them in a bag or hat to be drawn. Two people perform a scene from nothing (although the class may suggest a place or a relationship to get them started). One of the actors draws a subtext paper from the hat and must play that subtext throughout the scene without ever actually saying it. The other actor must attempt, through normal conversation, to figure out what the subtext is. For example, if the subtext is "I'm jealous of you," the other actor could guess by saying "You seem a little jealous of me right now." The teacher may end the scene by a certain time, or the scene can find its own natural ending. For fun, the audience may know the subtext and can give verbal cues to the actor guessing the subtext. When the subtext is correctly guessed, the audience (if they know it) can cheer to signify the end of the scene.

(Plus other previously mentioned exercises.)

Applying Dialect to a Role

Part of the fun in being an actor comes with the research I do for my roles. As one of my actor friends said, "I feel like I can write a thesis about Sweden, and I'm really just playing Miss Julie!" My enthusiasm for research has led me to devise a method for helping my students develop a comprehensive knowledge of the world of the character/accent. The best way to learn a consistent accent is to figure out why the character speaks the way he or she does. The student then becomes invested in creating a *person* rather than just a *sound change.*

In our character research process, the student asks him- or herself basic questions (adapted from Uta Hagen's list in *Respect for Acting*) that can reveal qualities needed for the accent:

- Who am I?
- Where am I?
- What am I?
- Who is around me?
- What is my past (immediate and ancient)?
- What is my future (impending and hopeful)?
- What time is it?
- What do I want in this play/scene?
- Why?
- What do I do to get what I want?

I encourage students to also ask themselves the following specific questions as part of the character-building process:

- What does/did my family do and how much money do I/we make?
- How is my health/energy?
- What is my self-image?
- What is my intellectual level?
- How do I walk?
- How do other people treat me?
- What is my status with the other people in the play/scene?
- What do other people say about me?
- What do I wish were true about me?
- What is my greatest fear?
- What is my greatest triumph?

- What kinds of music do I listen to?
- What do I do for fun?
- What is my religion?
- Where have I traveled?
- What do people in other places say about the way we talk here?
- How does my country/region stand in the great world picture?

Add your own questions!

FURTHER READING

Acting With An Accent and *Dialect Monologues* by David Alan Stern

The Actor and the Text by Patsy Rodenburg

The Actor Speaks by Patsy Rodenburg

Actor's Encyclopedia of Dialects by Donald Molin

American Dialectss and *Foreign Dialects* by Herman and Herman

"Dialect Notes" by Edith Skinner (note collection in A.C.T. library)

Dialects and Accents for Actors by Gillian Lane-Plescia

Dialects for the Stage and *Speech for the Stage* by Evangeline Machlin

The Dialect Handbook by Ginny Kopf

English Accents and Dialects by Hughes and Trudgill

"The History of English" PBS Documentary (video)

Impro by Keith Johnstone

The Joy of Phonetics and Accents by Louis Coloianni

The Need for Words by Patsy Rodenburg

The Right to Speak by Patsy Rodenburg

Speak With Distinction by Edith Skinner, Lilene Mansell and Timothy Monich

Stage Dialects and *More Stage Dialects* by Jerry Blunt

Vocal Direction for the Theatre: From Script Analysis

Voice and The Actor by Cicely Berry

To Opening Night by Nan Withers-Wilson

PERMISSIONS

Every effort has been made to locate the proper copyright holder for each excerpt published in this anthology. Any discrepancies or exclusions are unintentional.

CAUTION: Professionals and amateurs are hereby warned that performance of each excerpt is subject to royalty. It is fully protected under the copyright laws of the United States of America and of all countries covered by the International Copyright Union (including the Dominion of Canada and the rest of the British Commonwealth), and the Pan-American Copyright Convention, the Universal Copyright Convention, the Berne Convention, as well as all countries with which the United States has copyright relations. All rights, including professional and amateur stage rights, motion picture, recitation, lecturing, public reading, radio broadcasting, television, video or sound recording, all other forms of mechanical or electronic reproduction, such as CD-ROM, CD-1, information storage and retrieval systems and photocopying, and the rights of translation into foreign languages are strictly reserved. Particular emphasis is laid upon the matter of readings, permission for which must be obtained from the author's agent in writing.

Almost Grown by Richard Cameron. Copyright ©1994 by Richard Cameron. Reprinted by permission of Curtis Brown Group, Ltd. All inquiries should be addressed to: Curtis Brown Group, Ltd., Haymarket House, 4th Floor, 28/29 Haymarket, London, England, SW1Y 4SP.

A Bird of Prey by Jim Grimsley. Copyright ©1997 by Jim Grimsley., Reprinted by permission of the Author. All inquiries should be addressed to: The Gest Agency, 130 West 42nd Street, New York, NY 10036, Attn: Peter Hagan.

Blessed Assurance by Laddy Sartin. Copyright ©1992 by Laddy Sartin. Reprinted by permission of the Author. All inquiries should be addressed to: Harden-Curtis Associates, 850 Seventh Avenue, New York, NY 10016.

Boys' Life by Howard Korder. Copyright ©1988 by Howard Korder. Reprinted by permission of Grove/Atlantic, Inc. All inquiries should be addressed to: Dramatists Play Service, 400 Park Avenue South, New York, NY 10016.

Come Back to the Five & Ten, Jimmy Dean, Jimmy Dean by Ed Graczyk. Copyright ©1976, 1982 by Ed Graczyk. Reprinted by permission of Samuel French. All inquiries should be addressed to: Samuel French, 45 West 25th Street, New York, NY 10010-2751.

The Cripple of Inishmaan by Martin McDonagh. Copyright ©1997 by Martin McDonagh. Reprinted by permission of Methuen. All inquiries should be addressed to: Methuen, 215 Vauxhall Bridge Road, London, England, SW1V 1EJ.

Curse of the Starving Class by Sam Shepard. Copyright ©1976 by Sam Shepard. Reprinted by permission of Bantam Dell Publishing. All inquiries should be addressed to Bantam Dell Publishing, 1540 Broadway, New York, NY 10035.

Cyra and Rocky by Cherie Bennett. Copyright ©1997 by Cherie Bennett. Reprinted by permission of Dramatic Publishing. All inquiries should be sent to: Dramatic Publishing, 311 Washington St., Woodstock, IL 60098.

The Darker Face of the Earth by Rita Dove. Copyright ©1994, 1996 by Rita Dove. Reprinted by permission of the Author. All inquiries should be addressed to: Rita Dove, Dept. of English, Bryan Hall, University of VA, Charlottesville, VA 22903.

The Days and Nights of Beebee Fenstermaker by William Snyder. Copyright ©1963, renewed 1991 by William Snyder. Reprinted by permission of Flora Roberts Agency. All inquiries should be addressed to: Flora Roberts Agency, 157 West 57th Street, New York, NY 10019.

Early Dark by Reynolds Price. Copyright ©1977 by Reynolds Price. Reprinted by permission of Harriet Wasserman. All inquiries should be addressed to: Harriet Wasserman, 137 East 36th Street, New York, NY 10016.

Easy Access for the Boys by Claire Dowie. Copyright ©1998 by Claire Dowie. Reprinted by permission of Methuen. All inquiries should be addressed to: Methuen, 215 Vauxhall Bridge Road, London, England, SW1V 1EJ.

Girl Gone by Jacquelyn Reingold. Copyright ©1995 by Jacquelyn Reingold. Reprinted by permission of the Author. All inquiries for performance rights should be addressed to: Dramatists Play Service, 440 Park Avenue South, New York, NY 10016. For all other rights, please contact: Gersh Agency, 130 West 42nd Street, #2400, New York, NY 10036, Attn: Scott Toselow.

Goodnight Children, Everywhere by Richard Nelson. Copyright ©1997 by Richard Nelson. Reprinted by permission of Peter Franklin at the William Morris Agency. All inquiries should be addressed to: Broadway Play Publishing, 56 East 81st Street, New York, NY 10028.

Graceland by Ellen Byron. Copyright ©1982 by Ellen Byron. Reprinted by permission of the Author. All inquiries should be addressed to: Bret Adams, Ltd., 448 West 44th Street, New York, NY 10010.

A Hatful of Rain by Michael Gazo. Copyright ©1954, 1956, 1982, 1984 by Michael Gazo. Reprinted by permission of Samuel French. All inquiries should be sent to: Samuel French, 45 West 25th Street, New York, NY 10010.

The Indian Wants the Bronx by Israel Horowitz. Copyright ©1967 by Israel Horowitz. Reprinted by permission of Smith and Kraus Publishers. All inquiries should be addressed to: Smith and Kraus, P.O. Box 127, Lyme, NH 03768.

The Love-Girl and the Innocent by Aleksandr Solzhenitsyn. Copyright ©1969 by Aleksandr Solzhenitsyn. Reprinted by permission of Farrar, Straus and Giroux. All inquiries should be addressed to: Farrar, Straus and Giroux, LLC, 19 Union Square West, New York, NY 10003.

The Lovers by Brian Friel. Copyright ©1968 by Brian Friel. Reprinted by permission of the Author. All inquiries should be addressed to: The Agency, 24 Pottery Lane, Holland Park, London, England W11 4LZ.

Low Level Panic by Clare McIntyre. Copyright ©1989 by Clare McIntyre. Reprinted by permission of The Agency. All inquiries should be addressed to: The Agency, 24 Pottery Lane, Holland Park, London, England, W11 4LZ.

Marriage by Nikolai Gogol, adapted by Barbara Field. Copyright ©1987 by Barbara Field. Reprinted by permission of Dramatists Play Service. All inquiries should be addressed to: Dramatists Play Service, 440 Park Avenue South, New York, NY 10016.

The Mineola Twins by Paula Vogel. Copyright ©1997 by Paula Vogel. Reprinted by permission of Theatre Communications Group. All inquiries should be addressed to: TCG, 355 Lexington Avenue, New York, NY 10017.

The Monogamist by Christopher Kyle. Copyright ©1996 by Christopher Kyle. Reprinted by permission of the Joyce Ketay Agency. All inquiries should be addressed to: The Joyce Ketay Agency, 1501 Broadway, Suite 1908, New York, NY 10036.

Our Lady of Sligo by Sebastian Barry. Copyright ©1999 by Sebastian Barry. Reprinted by permission of Methuen. All inquiries should be addressed to: Methuen, 215 Vauxhall Bridge Road, London, England, SW1V 1EJ.

Ourselves Alone by Anne Devlin. Copyright ©1986, 1990, 1999 by Anne Devlin. Reprinted by permission of the Author and Dramatists Play Service. All inquiries should be addressed to: Dramatists Play Service, 440 Park Avenue South, New York, NY 10016.

Philadelphia, Here I Come by Brian Friel. Copyright ©1965 by Brian Friel. Reprinted by permission of Faber and Faber Limited. All inquiries should be addressed to: Faber and Faber Limited, 3 Queen Square, London, England, WC1N 3AU.

The Piano Lesson by August Wilson. Copyright ©1988, 1990 by August Wilson. Reprinted by permission of Dutton Signet, a division of Penguin Putnam, Inc. All inquiries should be addressed to: Penguin Putnam, Inc., 375 Hudson Street, New York, NY 10014.

Quartermaine's Terms by Simon Gray. Copyright ©1981, 1983 by Simon Gray. First published in 1981 by Eyre Methuen Ltd. Reprinted by permission of the Author. All inquiries should be addressed to: Judy Daish Associates, 2 Street Charles Place, London, England W10 6EG.

SPECIAL THANKS AND ACKNOWLEDGMENTS

*A.C.T.'s MFA class of 1995, Kate Brickley, Elizabeth Brodersen,
Lia Fischer, Elaine Foreman, Jeffrey Draper, Jennifer Gould,
Kat Koppett, Gillian Lane-Plescia, Domenique Lozano,
Carey Perloff, Pamela Ricard, Joe Rosenthal,
Jack Sharrar, Craig Slaight,
Melissa Smith, John Sugden, Deborah Sussel,
Francine Torres-Kelly, V.A.S.T.A., Gemma Whelan,
All the young conservatory students at A.C.T., and
Dave Hill, the love of my life.*